# THE VOICE

## BEHIND THE CURTAIN

# THE VOICE

## BEHIND THE CURTAIN

WARRIOR ZUZU

PARTRIDGE
A Penguin Random House Company

**To order additional copies of this book, contact**
Toll Free 0800 990 914 (South Africa)
+44 20 3014 3997 (outside South Africa)
orders.africa@partridgepublishing.com

www.partridgepublishing.com/africa

We bleed to survive then we survive just to bleed again, because we are in the race of survival. I am a warrior—but so are you.

Warrior Zuzu

Some names in this book are changed to protect those who are still alive.

# INTRODUCTION

There is a voice behind the curtain, and it is the voice of Annie Anonyma, the little girl with the vivid imagination who loves to read. Annie Anonyma believes that her imagination is her most powerful force. Her face carries an invisible mask as she hides behind the curtain. But, her spirit and resilience for life is remarkable no matter what the circumstances. To Annie, change is not only possible but also probable. Her fears, she believes, are what will make her strong to overcome adversity. Furthermore, her emotional and physical suffering will come to a dead end. She will be free and loved, and then she will live life to the fullest. There will be a date, a time and a place—then with a brave heart she will step into her greatness. The world will then meet her for the first time and see the beauty within. She will show the passion of her soul and the world will embrace her with love and respect. For now, it is all about time for only time knows the set of terms while she is fighting the physical and emotional challenges throughout her insipid childhood.

The voice was silent for too many years and now the time has arrived for this voice to be heard. Annie is a person who will tell the story as she remembers. This book is her voice, her platform, and now is the time. This work will bring exceptional healing to her soul. All the associations and memories will guide her through her way to execute this project. Breaking the silence of her painful memories and sad emotions of fear, anxiety, and anger will do her a great justice that will last forever. She will be detached from the circumstances and the misery that has no purpose or value in her life. Her faith is pinned on what she believes and that is the human spirit within shall never die while she is alive. The challenge is to conquer the emotional pain of a toxic past. She will remember that from her childhood, she nurtured the good seed. By doing that, she learned to forgive and love and turn away from blame and anger. No longer will the dark cloud of misery be the opiate of her thoughts.

I urge you to venture with me on an interesting journey and lend an ear to hear the voice before she removes the invisible mask.

# PROLOGUE

Gazing at the crimson sky as she patiently waits for the epic moment, Annie Anonyma, the daughter of Nellie, is pleased with everything about nature. Soon the sun will set and she is waiting to be captivated in the moment. She wishes that she could grow up sooner. Her mission is to fight against all odds. To begin with, her childhood life is harsh with that ruffian of a stepfather but Annie will survive because she is in the world where the survivor of the fittest counts. After all, she has an amazing bold imagination and can create a special world for herself, by using her powerful imagination. The little girl believes that her imagination is her powerhouse. Therefore, she does not allow any negative factor to come between her and her daydreams. Besides, her spirit and resilience are remarkable. That is to say, she works hard on her mind to remain sane.

Annie was born under the star sign Libra, with the result that she does not like her balance to be disrupted with negative thoughts.

This is her moment when she enjoys peace and a calm assurance. Therefore, she enters into her peaceful zone, awaiting the presentation of nature's beauty as the day will turn away. This moment is not make-believe. This is reality and a definite instant playing out—the release of nature's action. Should anyone dare to invade her concentration now, she would fight him or her with immense silence.

For a second she looks down then her gaze goes back to the pristine sky and it pleases her prevailing psychological state.

The sunrays are softly melting as they interact with the clouds, forming an amazing colour combination of different yellows and orange. As the sun prepares to resign from the African sky for the day—she gets ready to become one with it. To her it is all about the skies' amazing blanket of beauty; nothing else matters—at least for now. She is captivated and hypnotized in this super moment and it is an effective platform. It is hers and only hers alone. Infused with what plays out, she watches with great appreciation. It is her distinctive emotional aura. Nothing can invade the peaceful offering of this special moment because her world is wide now with the highest saturation. Standing in silent obedience as if it is a ritual—her fixed paternal gaze lasts until she could see the sun no more. Then with closed eyes she whispers softly thanking the Creator for the creation and opens her eyes again in great appreciation, pleased but quite aware that tomorrow morning her gaze will be to the east for sunrise.

But later tonight when she has to lock the gate, she will have a minute or two to see the stars. Annie believes that the stars will watch over her while she sleeps. To her, this is life and these little moments are what write the pages of her history.

In addition to this life, Annie has so many questions but there is no one to answer them or should one say there are no answers. For now she is only a voice behind a curtain, but one day the voice will have a platform and a face. Then it will be a rebirth. The curtain will be drawn, and the voice will come out from behind the curtain to be heard. Yes, the voice will break the silence that was hidden in the dark. The stage will be set, and the voice will then speak with an austere quality yet be timid in a special way.

Every question will have an answer and every action will have a reason. As for the invisible mask, it will be removed from the face of the voice, to display victory. The enthusiasm of a new being will then have depth for a new walk—a new life.

However, her biggest question is, Why is this man whom her mother chose to be her father so unkind to her? Is it supposed to be like that? There is no one to answer but she is fine with it. In fact, there will be many more questions to come as the years go by.

At any rate, soon it will be dark and then her stepfather, whom she refers to as her stepdad, will be home. If her chores of the day are not according to his specification, then it will mean trouble for her. His black genuine-leather belt will be in action to leave bruises on her body. In silence and immense concentration, she goes through her list that she made to double-check. Yes, everything is in order, but will her stepdad be satisfied? Just thinking about him causes tension in her tummy.

Nevertheless, it has become second nature to Annie to follow a pattern of eating her supper in a rush so that she can be out of the kitchen before he makes his appearance and starts to shout with blustered authority. The scared little girl can't stand his abuse and grumpy attitude towards her. As for his eyes, oh, those big red eyes look like they can pop out of their sockets any time. Those eyes make her so scared although they hide behind the thick glass of his spectacles. If he removes those spectacles, he is as blind as a bat. It is indeed a fact that Annie fears her stepfather.

During the week, he is calmer but come Fridays then all hell breaks loose, especially when he comes home drunk. Not only does the flow of insults come easily from his mouth—no, he is also fast with lifting his hands. By Monday, her mother would sometimes have a black eye, bruises, and many marks of abuse on her body. Weekends were really a time that Annie did not look forward to. If only the days, weeks, months, and years could pass faster for her to be an adult away from this house and this life with this man.

Quietly she walks to her room and set herself on her favourite chair in the corner. It is better for her to avoid the kitchen so that she does not have to see the man that has no love for her. Listening with an attentive ear, she heard his authoritative voice as he loudly speaks to her mother. The tension in her stomach made her feel nauseous.

'Did that brat do everything I told her to do or was she again lazy?' He blustered with agitation.

'Yes, she did all her chores,' her mother replies in a very disciplined way. Annie crossed her fingers, hoping and praying that he would not call her for questioning. She waited in anticipation to hear if he would call her, but he didn't. Instead he started chatting with Nellie about his day at work. This time Annie escaped her stepfather's confrontation.

And later on, when he leaves the kitchen, she will slip out to go and lock the gate when he is in bed. Tomorrow morning she will be up at five to open it again. At least it is not so cold these days, but during the winter month, the chain is all iced up and then it is a real struggle with the lock. Her mother usually mixes the hot water to make it lukewarm to wash the ice from the windscreen of his van. The warm water makes it easy for Annie to remove the ice. The father in the house is the king and he must be served like a king. Polished shoes, clean van, and even his peanuts must never have the red skin on, not even one.

The truth is, if his things are not in order the way he wants it, then Annie becomes the prime target of his genuine-leather belt. Therefore, she adheres to all chores given by the king. Above all, she would never dare to question his authority or even risk repudiating his rules. Living under his roof means a set of strict rules shall be obeyed.

This is her life between the walls of a home with a noxious atmosphere where no love is present. However, these are the four walls that Annie says she did not build. By the time she was old enough to understand, she simply found herself within these walls. Generally speaking, it is a continuous fight to keep the peace just to get through another day. She sees herself as a warrior on the battlefield, fighting hard to survive. She bleeds every day from the inside out, and she is the only one that sees the invisible blood. She will remain the warrior, and the warrior must stand tall and survive. Yes, in her eyes it is her war and a war she cannot escape for now. But, the day will come when this war will reach its end.

# CHAPTER 1

The nervous little girl knows how to create her own way of escape from this painful era that she lives in. For balance, reading is what she enjoys. As a rule, she consumes many books and lives in the stories she reads. This way it became habitual for her to sway away from her intricacies. By and large, the vivid imagination that she has is her greatest asset. For this reason, it allows her to dream and build her own little castles. At the same time, with this powerful imagination, she dares to dream big and all her dreams are eminent to her. She is on her own path and no one has the right to divert it. Therefore, she rules her thoughts with supremacy and nothing can contain her. In short, what she dreams and holds in her subconscious mind her stepfather cannot put his hands on. Despite all the obstacles, it is an exceptional honour for her to know that she is in possession of this great degree of power.

She alone can change the rules and the specifications of the building plan of her future. Yes, a fearless future she will have one day when she is all grown up. For now her stepfather is the big bad wolf and she is the frail little Red Riding Hood. He huffs and he puffs, gives orders, and screams at her with aggravating aggression—like a lunatic with no limitations. Only he enjoys what he is doing to her and her mother says nothing. Nevertheless, she believes that one day his huffing and puffing will fall silent.

Consequently, for now she has great hopes and dreams and that is what keeps her going. It is the hopes and dreams to be a *somebody* one day. Her stepfather continually reminds her that she is a nothing with no identity or belonging, a fatherless child. Hence, the cruel man's words do hurt but she knows how to dismiss the negative from her way of thinking. With acclaimed faith, she knows that one day she will be successful and married to a good man. It is nice for her to think that one day she will have kids of her own whom she will love and protect with her life. Furthermore, what she dreams is not just sandcastles she is formulating in her mind; no, she is determined to make every dream a reality—it will be a turning point.

With a different outlook on life, she does not think like her peers who want to become doctors and scientists. No, Annie thinks of becoming a writer because reading is her passion. In contrast, writing down what she feels is her asset of a special kind. In essence, that is how she can free herself from many emotional unpleasant scenes—scenes like the genuine-leather belt that is a frequent guest that always makes contact with her body. Or a day she can recall when her stepdad sent her to the shop to buy cigarettes. She took too long according to him, and he took a walk to the shop and gave her a hiding in front of everyone. At least for that matter, no one laughed at her, and the shopkeeper warned him that she would report him to child welfare. Annie was so embarrassed that night, and sleep did not come easy. Being embarrassed was one thing, but what was worse was the confusion she had to deal with, the same faces she would come across in the shop again. Would all those people stare at her and think that she was a disobedient child? What if they laughed at her and called her names?

Nevertheless, one night he had the nerve to send her to the shop at night alone, and she had to cross an open veldt. Her stepfather knew that it was gangster territory and that it was unsafe for anyone to walk that way alone, how much more a ten-year-old girl. What was wrong with his thinking? Again the confusion, maybe one day she would understand. Maybe, one day it would all make sense. But would that day ever come?

As she walked in fear, she prayed and asked God to protect her. Many things went through her mind as reality was closing in. Did this man want something bad to happen to her—and why did her mother allow this?

Why couldn't she protect her or just speak out against his violent manner? What gave him the right to compromise her safety?

Withstanding such intense emotional feelings, it breaks her heart to think that her mother does not care and she feels lost, unprotected, and alone. Not even an animal gets so much punishment. However, she knows that one day there will be a reward for this penalty.

She realized that evil people like him do exist in this world and think that their power is absolute. However, she knew in her heart one day he would meet his day, she vowed to herself. The world is big and round. As for this aggressive man, there would come a day for him to know that there is a God.

For what he does to her and her mom, he will pay a massive price. Not that she is cursing him but that is how it works—what you sow, you shall reap. The Bible says so and the Bible is the ultimate book she so often reads. At least, most of her answers come from the Bible.

Anyway, by the time she got to the gate, her mother was standing and waiting for her, glad to see that her daughter was safe and sound. That night Annie could not read the Bible like she usually did, because she went to bed in a state of sadness. This sadness carried much more deepness. She looked at the Bible on the bedside pedestal but felt disappointed, with cluttered emotions, thinking in her heart, why did God allow this cruelty to wound her so much? For a moment she wished that she could be outside to hug her peach tree and feel the heat from its stump. Burdened and grieved, she silently fell asleep as tears rolled down her face.

The Saturday of that week was not a glorious weekend at all. Her stepfather did not go to work and it was a horrific day for Annie. He woke her early and told her it was the day for garden inspection, and his van needed a good cleaning. He made his inspection and his findings were as usual—he was not satisfied. Not that it should be a surprise, no, he was and always would be negative about everything Annie did.

What she did in the week with the garden she had to do over according to his requirements. He gave instructions like a military officer and it was quite maddening. Yet it came across as a joke to Annie. His voice was irritating and a hindrance to her soul. However, in her heart she was laughing because he sounded doltish.

At times she is not sure if she should remain calm while he is raising his voice using the most unrefined words. It is evident that the two of them share different opinions about gardening and he always lacks appreciation. At any rate, Annie hates it when he calls her stupid because right now he is the one sounding stupid. She decides against a slip of the tongue, knowing that she will get a fierce blow against her head. He is very fast with his backhand.

Instead, she rakes the soil but with abundance of her love. In her heart she claims the soil to be hers. Not in the least is it senseless, what she is doing to the soil. She loves doing what she has to do because he looks at it as punishment but she takes it as a time of nurturing. On the other hand, she feels well advanced to his thinking and criticism. While he is undermining the work of her hands, she trains her mind to unleash her full potential—she connects with her silence. The secret now is to have a bonding session with the soil that she is tilling. Give him his due, she thinks to herself; he wants to be the man in control, but one day the element of surprise will step in. That is when he will have no say and no control over her life. The interpretation is his life will no longer be so jaunty because his victim will be gone and grown up. For now he is only a voice that utters words of abuse. But the day will come when her voice will have a platform. Let the big bad wolf huff and puff as much as he likes, because the ears of Little Red Riding Hood do not respond. The counter-secret is she will not allow him to dissolve her powerful way of thinking. The methods of his punishment are harsh and his insults are demeaning but it will never break down the spirit of her perseverance. With good character, she complies with every instruction he gives, knowing that one day there will be a compensation for her—a better life.

She disregards the sound of his voice as she interacts with the garden rake—pushing it forward and pulling it backward. At the same time, the movement is toning her arms. How blessed is she for getting a double portion, bonding and toning. With great intensity she concentrates on the gravity of the moment. It feels good because she knows that she is about to win the contest.

When he realized that he was only wasting his time trying so hard to break her spirit, he walked away like a loser. Not surprised, yet satisfied, Annie knew in her heart that her strong spirit has stopped the duel and that makes her the clear winner. Why is she the winner? She is the winner for transforming this exercise into a positive situation. Not to prove a point to him but to prove to her that she indeed has a brilliant mind and for those who does not believe it, they can ask the universe. With great appreciation, Annie felt like laughing but refrained from the thought. For now she was brimming with victory and happy to continue with her chores. When she was done with the garden, she washed and polished his van.

Nevertheless, it is not easy for a ten-year-old to forget, given the many flashbacks that would occasionally come alive and haunt her mind. Of note was the one night she had to see how her stepfather tried to hit her mom with an axe while she was lying sick in bed. It was by the grace of God that her mother managed to be fast enough. Just in time, Nellie moved her head to the other side and the axe went right into the headboard and left a vicious mark. Truly speaking, that mark was a sign of his anger, as from that day, Annie made it her duty to hide the axe under her bed behind a suitcase. The point is, she knew that her stepdad would never look for it because he never chopped wood. However, when the ruthless man realized what he just did, he sort of came to his senses and walked out of the room without an apology.

Whenever he displays stunts like these, it is as if a demonic force takes over his body. As a result, then he sees nothing and feels nothing. Can it be that he is truly a man without a soul or is he just ignorant? All this emotional and physical stress is tormenting little Annie. She knows that her mom too suffers with the stress but her choice is to stick around. Over the years, her mother became his emotional hostage. Sadly, it is a decision Annie cannot change.

When Nellie was two months pregnant, he kicked her and she lost the baby. But the most painful one was the day he called Annie to give her a piece of his chocolate. Annie had to kneel before him like a beggar to receive the chocolate she never even asked for. It would be a massive understatement to say that his behaviour that night was infantile—it was unkind and inhuman.

'Take!' he yelled at Annie. With nervousness and a shivering little hand she reached out to take the piece of chocolate but before she could even thank him, he yelled.

'Say thank you, ungrateful little rubbish!' he yelled again with authoritative bluster and with his eyes so big it instantly made Annie want to cry.

'Thank you, Daddy,' Annie whispered with a trembling voice.

'Don't say Daddy, I am not your daddy . . . say thank you, dog,' he yelled with so much hatred in his voice.

'No, Daddy,' she answered with a pleading voice.

'I said, "Say thank you, dog"!' This time his yelling was more intense; he screamed like a deranged man, commanding the child, 'Say thank you, dog,' and in a confused state of mind, she said it.

'What did you say?' And in his bewildered rage, he hit Annie with the back of his hand in her face. She flew from her knees and landed on the cold floor close to the coal stove. The piece of chocolate was melting and fell out of her now-swollen hand because it hit against the stove. Nellie looked on but said nothing. They lived in a four-room council house; the kitchen, two bedrooms and a lounge, and all the rooms were compact. The houses were built in such a way for the non-whites. It was the way of the apartheid regime.

Nellie got up from where she was sitting and walked out. That made the king of the castle angrier and fiercer. He got up from his chair, grabbed her and pulled her by the hair, and dragged her back into the kitchen.

'Woman, don't you dare walk out when I discipline your child!'

'That is not discipline, that is abuse!' she yelled back at him.

Answering back was a bad mistake that Nellie made but Annie was surprised to see her mother's retaliation. The king smacked her in the same way he did her daughter, and she fell onto the stove and knocked her forehead against the plate of the coal stove. As a consequence, a loud cry came from Nellie's mouth, and in the blink of an eye, a painful-looking bruise was noticeable. The stove was still hot, was the first thought running through Annie's mind. Fearfully and with tears in her eyes, sitting on one side of the kitchen floor, close to her mother, she watched. Watching what was transpiring, feeling so helpless and demeaned, she looked on. The burning sting of the smack in her face she could still feel. Every move he made she watched, and she was very cautious for his next move, quite aware that he was a dangerous man when in this mood. But he was now on her mother's case. She was relieved for the small break but dared not leave the kitchen now. Unsympathetically, he started shouting and cursing, telling his wife how she and her whore child did not appreciate what he did for them. It was from insult to insult. From living under his roof, eating his food, enjoying all the facilities he provided was what they had to hear. But he mentioned nothing about all the chores he gave or how he treated and disrespected them. He applauded himself and felt good about it.

'You and your whore child are nothing and you come from nothing, and now you get too used to everything and want to have attitude with me. I work and give both of you everything. I demand respect because this is my house and I pay for everything. There is your brat sitting!' He pointed at Annie. 'Her so-called father denied her and I took her in. I feed her, clothe her, educate the stupid thing and pay for whatever she is in need of, and no appreciation from any of you swines. Your lives are nothing without me.'

On his face was a look of great satisfaction for saying what he said. His wife knew his ways; it was time to rather say nothing or she would get it again. The indecent language he used against them was beyond human explanation. For a quick moment, Annie looked at this brutal man, she summed him up: the violent look in his eyes and evil demeanour. He is the epitome of a grisly sight because his résumé is not short of brutality. She looked at a man with no heart, no conscience, and no soul. He was ruthless, mean, and evil.

Rudely awoken from her thoughts, she had to see yet another blow with his big rough hand landing on her mother's face. He turned to Annie and gave her an unfriendly look—a look that said, 'I despise you'.

Annie found his ego very annoying and offensive, but said nothing. What would she say anyway? She had no human rights to say anything. As for him, he was the tormentor who had no feelings for the next person, and for now he reigned with an iron hand. All of this was not only sinful but also traumatic and degrading.

Still and all, it was a long night of verbal and physical abuse. The angry mean man did not have enough yet and grabbed Annie—yelling, pulling her hair, and screaming in her ear that she must go look for her father. He then pushed them out through the kitchen door, on that cold night, using the very bad language he so proudly used to degrade and intimidate them.

As it is, barring her thoughts, this young child with so many hidden emotional pains has big hopes for her future. She prays every night to the Almighty God to take care of her destiny. Besides, she has placed all her confidence in her Divine Father's timing, believing that He knows best, considering when that time comes, then the wings of her spirit will be set free. Because of what she sees and has to bear, she sometimes can't help thinking and wondering what life would have been for her with her biological father. Generally speaking, it is a painful thought and it does hurt. However, for now life is only a sacrifice with a selfish man whom she is forced to call father.

The fact of the matter is, sometimes single mothers seek love and think they found it when a man comes into their lives. Needless to say, they are suddenly in a comfortable place with financial support. Of course, some men even get married to them. Then sadly they have to pay a price because these men own them, as they become the victims of all kinds of abuse, like the scenario which her mother happens to find herself in. Not all men are like that; there are good men on this earth. Amusingly, Annie pacifies herself by thinking maybe if she lived with her own father, she was not going to appreciate nature the way she does. Right now nature is her friend, and her love for this friend teaches her to truly accept life for the way it is now. In simple terms, nature is her sanity and her sanity is her hope. Hope and faith are what she depends on for her future—her hope she must keep alive. This broken child with the lumbering childhood shook her head and quickly changed her thoughts like one would change a nasty topic.

To summarize, every time her mind runs riot, she makes it her duty to defend her ground. In short, it is to remain at peace and not lose hope. Because of lifelike images within her mind, she looks at the world in a different way, always comparing it with some of the stories in the various books she reads. Her brain will always be engendered with the awful flashbacks of her own screams and tears while all the pain was inflicted with cursing and insults. That is why she never reads or watches horror, not even in the comic books. Yes, it is true that in some people's minds, evil neither slumbers nor sleeps.

Above all the adverse things, Annie is also a great sprinter and is always active in the school sports at the beginning of each school year. Sprinting is good for her, because when she sprints she imagines herself running with the horses. If only she could run away with them forever, to be in a place where the big bad wolf does not exist. That is why it is so important for her to watch the beautiful sunsets—because then the big bad wolf is of no existence to her. That is to say, the universe occupies her mind and she enjoys a world of her own—without the blasting of a cruel man.

Finally, she cannot wait for tomorrow, it is the first day of the school holidays and then she can play with her babies Tania and Andy. They are the neighbour's children and she loves them like they are her sister and brother. It is like a custom that they will sleep over from tomorrow. At least her stepfather doesn't mind when they are there. He has no children with Nellie; that is why he likes to have Andy and Tania around. Anyway, these two children are like a crutch for Annie to lean on.

Having these two around always puts Annie in a state of sublime happiness. They sit quietly when Annie reads to them. They enter into her world of colour and nature with all the beautiful animals; she shows them the pictures in the books. Sometimes puzzled but eager, they enter with Annie into her animated fantasy world.

Above all, she likes it when she gives them the oranges that she cuts up. She watches them eating and laughs because the juice runs down their arms and drips from their little elbows. Needless to say, for Annie this is a classic picture. The two little ones love Annie because she is always so caring and patient with them, and when they fall and hurt themselves, Annie would kiss it better for the pain to go away. It is important for her when Tania and Andy sleep over then she is not alone. In addition, it helps her not to think too much about her heartaches, taking into account that sometimes she has to bribe them by promising to read stories from a new library book.

One day her own story will be in a book but she will write it herself. Life is a story and this world is one big library. Every human walking the earth has a memoir somewhere in the library of the universe. Not all stories are sad but we all have a story to tell. Every story starts with the day we enter Earth. Therefore, every story ends the day we die. The memory may live on but the memoir is complete. Although Annie's story is sad, it will have a good ending and her legacy will remain.

One Saturday night Tania slept over, and the king was in a good mood because he won some money on horse racing. He was arrogant about his winnings but at least he was in a good mood. Money made sense to him—it made him happy. His good mood meant a chill-out time for Annie. He had a few beers but was not at all drunk. Nellie made his favourite food, and all his favourites were as bland as he was, not the kind of veggies children would appreciate. It was boiled broccoli, carrots, Brussels sprouts lightly peppered with rice, and stew. To him it was a meal fit for a king but then again for the kind of king he is, he deserved to eat that way. As for Tania, she was one child who knew how to impress him and gave him plenty of compliments about his healthy way of eating. The ego of the king went from zero to ten, and he instructed Nellie to dish more veggies for Tania. On the other hand, Tania was fooling around and told him that she admired him a lot because he was a man with high standards. Annie looked at Tania and the naughty girl gave her a quick wink with the eye. Without any question, Annie got the message and smiled. Anyway, the night went well off, and they watched a movie that he liked. It wasn't long, and then Tania lost interest and fell asleep. The king of the cave too went to his bed. It was only a pleasure for Annie to carry Tania to bed. Nonetheless, it was a task to take off Tania's gown before putting her into bed. Annie managed well and standing with the gown in her hand she could not contain her emotions. She burst out laughing. The king already dozed off and Nellie came to Annie's room to investigate what the commotion was. Still laughing Annie showed her mother the pockets of Tania's gown and they both went into a choir of laughter. Tania's gown pockets were stuffed with broccoli, carrots, and Brussels sprouts. And yet she was complimenting the king through the meal about the great vitamins and nutrition and how good these veggies are for the human body. Annie looked at the sleeping innocent face on the bed and said, 'That is why I love you so much, you know how to make me laugh.'

Regardless of how Tania might be a few years younger, she is a support system to Annie. To Annie, Tania is her little sister; she leans on her yet Tania is too young to know or even understand—but maybe one day she will hear it herself. Be that as it may, her stepdad sometimes plays with Tania and Andy, and it makes Annie wonder why he can't be like that to her. What has she done to make him despise her so much? Another question with vain expectations and no answer but to Annie it is fine. Maybe, *just maybe*, one day he will change and accept her as his own child; whether it will happen remains to be seen.

# Chapter 2

One Monday afternoon, Annie noticed the sad look on her mother's face. That look, oh, that look touched her and she knew why. Her mom's arms were covered in purplish bruises and Annie did not even want to recall what she saw over the past weekend. Primarily, it was better for her to simply block certain snippets from her mind. She sat on the first step of the stoep and looked in the direction where her mother was sitting on the chair. Nellie was still looking at the same spot, saying nothing, and a teardrop fell from her swollen bruised eye. Annie looked up to the bright sky and quietly asked God, why did he allow all this? In turn, the girl in pigtails felt so helpless and wished her mom could just say something to break the silence, but she said nothing. In the meantime, Annie thought to herself, trying to mitigate. She focused on the words rumbling in her mind, 'one day all this will be over and I will give my mother a better life and home'. But for now they both just had to deal with the invisible shackles around their ankles. Despondent, she sighed as if the whole world was coming to an end.

Nevertheless, Annie has two friends living down the road and they too have a stepfather but he loves them to bits as if they were his own children. He plays with them on the lawn and showers them with chocolate on paydays. They always share their chocolate with Annie when she is around, playing with them. They would brag and tell her that they sit on their papa's lap and talk about what they did at school, especially if some of the kids have tried to bully them. Annie does not know what it's like to sit on a daddy's lap and complain about a day that went wrong. At least, no one will ever bully her because she has built up a self-defence mechanism whereby she protects herself. Her tongue is that weapon of defence, and because she is a reader, she knows how to use words and defend herself. She knows no daddy to fend for her. She only knows how to polish his shoes, wash his car, change the car wheels, and look after the vegetable garden she made—that he claims to be his. She only knows authoritative instructions blustered out that she has to adhere to. However, all these tasks are her lessons she gets now for the future and she does not mind anymore. For now it is a prescribed textbook. However, it is only evident that one day she will be self-sufficient because her prescribed textbook will be her tool book.

The fact is, her so-called daddy does not even care about her schooling. Currently, to him she is just a brat. For the most part, that is what he always calls her and she does not like it. As one would expect, she looked up the word *brat* in the dictionary and saw the meaning, and it did not please her at all. For one thing, she is no one's brat and that is a fact. He might call her a brat, forgetting in her eyes he is Mr Whiplash.

To Annie this world is truly a strange place; again she gazes up to the sky with a desire to know if it is the same up there. It is obvious that she is aware of the planets behind the clouds; she read about it in a book. Nevertheless, it makes her wonder if there are people on those planets and if they are cruel or loving. Her enquiring mind wants to know, Do they read books, eat, and sleep, and are they like humans? One day when she is on her own, the face of this cruel man will be but a fading memory of a past she would never want to remember. But will the past leave her in peace or will the past follow her like a shadow? Besides, will the past even disturb her in her sleep with unpleasant dreams? In this case, she hopes that the past will have no interest in her at all. Recurrently, she knows it all depends on time because time is always on time.

Again, she is pestered with too many inconvenient questions and no one to answer. Currently, she became accustomed to the fact that she cannot voice her concerns to anyone. It is a matter of course that she is the only voice she knows. There are no ears to listen and no mouths to speak up. Her peculiar mind knows that. However, she cannot halt the forward march of the great life that is awaiting her. Therefore, she needs to be in control of her faculties. It is a matter of becoming the manager of all her emotions. In truth, one day the good has to overshadow the evil and she will be strong enough to face the world on her own as an adult. At the same time, love will prevail in her life because she has enough of that to give. Right now she has to cope with the unfortunate complications. No means of escape for now, all that is left is time. Why, because time says nothing yet everything. For the time being, what she needs to do is to embrace the present and merge with it for the sake of her stability. After all, reality has no special time; it goes from day to day and it is what it is for now. With this in mind, her strength she will preserve to accomplish the goals set out for her future, not forgetting that she has the stars in the night sky to talk to and in the morning she can give her peach tree a hug and feel the energy of its stump. Then, late afternoon there is always a sunset. And even if it rains, then the promise of God will be in the sky in the form of a rainbow. So as a final analysis, to every negative there is a positive. Life is what one makes of it because life wants to be lived—for now she is living. No matter what one faces in life, one should never let go of hope.

To say the least, Annie tries every day to walk tall and be strong but she is only a child trying to be brave, knowing that the habit of her persistence will one day make her see victory and freedom. However, she also fears that she might break. Her little body is not designed to withstand all this strain, and the growing pressure is starting to interfere with her mental confidence. Sometimes it's hard for her to even concentrate at school. Will her body cope with all this talk or will her mind just give up one day? Like her granny always says, *talk is cheap*. In spite of all these emotions, she is not talking; she is thinking, and her brain likes it and won't give up on her. But deep down in her subconscious, a few things should seriously be eradicated; indeed it is not easy. In turn, one's past is not always friendly; it can come up with violent turbulence.

Many afternoons after school, she would interrogate her mother, trying to understand, why do they have to remain in this situation? Particularly with a man that is so cruel and disagreeable with them. As usual, her mother would encourage her to get educated, and after she passed matric, they will take an out. Her mother explained to her at length that she was in this position because of the lack of education and not being self-sustainable.

'My child,' she said, and her facial appearance was serious when she added, 'All women must be educated and have skills to do something. I will never see you making the same mistakes I did. When a woman is educated, she is empowered and knows her self-worth.'

Astounded by words that made perfect sense, Annie looked at her mom, and it was as if it all opened up to her. Her mother was reliant on this man. He earned the money, and her mother was the slave he could push around as he pleased. She knew now that her mother had no say because the ruthless man paid for them to live what he thought was a solid life.

'Wow,' Annie whispered, '*how messed up.*'

After hearing what her mother said, she felt really obligated to be under strict subjection. Her mother did not get out because she wanted her to be educated. Annie's eyes warmed up; she was close to tears because she felt guilty for putting her mother through all of this havoc. As an illustration, there is no way her mom would get a job without being educated and without skills. Her mother was holding on to her purpose and was not prepared to give in. It was obvious that she preferred to go through this abuse because of her child. Together with this information, Annie tried to analyze this situation of sacrifice.

Is it selfish, necessary, and worthwhile, or is it misunderstood? Or is her mother so confused and indoctrinated by this evil man's ways that she uses her child as a scapegoat to stay in a loveless marriage? All this is not easy for the ten-year-old girl to understand. Consequently, the pains of betrayal presented with facts run deep now.

'Why, Lord, why?' Annie whispered.

'One day . . . be patient,' Annie's mother whispered back.

How long would she be in this prison of bondage, where it was impossible for her to enjoy her childhood? It was sad for her to hear that they have to wait for a few more years, years of physical and verbal abuse, and the fact that her mother was subdued to this unhappy marriage. To begin with, it sounded like a never-ending pandemic. In question was, would she be able to manage all the stress without collapse? Most of the time it was so hard for her to cope with her studies because of the constant fights against the restraints of duty and its accompanying decorum he gave her. Nevertheless, she needed to hold on because for her to obtain matric one day was vital and she was only in primary school now, a long way from the freedom she so often longed for.

This is her life for now and the way to conquer all the chaos is to simply break it up into small pieces and just let go and live. She will always remember her mother's words. It might not be easy but there is no other choice, unless her mother makes a move. However, these conditions are extremely sensitive and painful but some day it has to end. It is so simple because they can leave here and live with her grandmother, but her mother would hear nothing of that. That is why the husband thinks he has his wife in the palm of his hand. The fact is, she has a mother whose mind is incarcerated. However, Annie's mother explains to her that she made a vow and it is in sickness and in health, for better and for worse. But what her mother does not understand is that she made the vow—now why must Annie suffer under the rules of her vow? Is this one of those things they say—it's life? And if so then it is a very unfair life, that is for sure, but truly it won't be for keeps.

# CHAPTER 3

It is a beautiful sunny Sunday afternoon, a perfect day for tennis, Annie thought. Usually on Sunday afternoons her stepfather takes his afternoon nap. He gets easily offended if any noise causes a disturbance when he is resting, therefore he does not mind when the little brat is not around. At least she washed his van early morning and cleaned the inside so that he goes to work with a clean vehicle because he always brags that he is the boss on site.

'Mr Boss,' Annie would always whisper and secretly laugh when he was not looking.

'Who would want to have such an ugly boss, with his Coca-Cola-bottle spectacles, blind bat, and do his friends and staff know about the jam between his toes, with his smelly size-ten bunion feet . . . but he is a boss.'

Nonetheless, earlier on he ordered with his usual authority how Annie should not miss a spot when she polished the spokes of every wheel.

'Oh gosh,' Annie would quietly whisper, thinking how self-centred and high-maintenance he and wondering, does his workforce know that this ugly man is a woman beater? She wondered, where did her mother meet this ugly mean machine with his knock knees and super-big nostrils similar to those of a horse after a race. *This man is worse than JR in the soapy* Dallas.

Annie was three years old when her mother left her granny to live with him and later they got married. Granny wanted Annie but her mother would not leave without her child. Therefore she is now caged in this situation.

To say life is unfair would be a great understatement. She realizes that it is not life that brings pain and fear. It is humans that walk the earth but not all. There will always be mischief, dishonesty, and many more storms that will create all kinds of emotions. Her existence in this world she will never regard as incongruous. It would be ungrateful of her to even think that way because life is a gift from God. To give up on life is what she would call unfair. It is her belief that all are here to fulfil a purpose no matter how unfavourable or sad, the journey one must travel until the end. Every Earth dweller has a purpose.

That day she spent hours on the tennis court with her two friends down from her street. Her friends would always go out of their way to make her laugh. They were aware of the situation at Annie's home. All the same, they tried not to talk about it too much because it would only bring discomfort to Annie. On several occasions when the topic came up, they noticed the sad facial expression that would dismiss the smile of their friend's face, and Annie's smile is so delightful. There is just something in that smile because it serves as a mask of what she is hiding. Therefore, that topic is a no go unless Annie brings it up which she never does.

Later that afternoon after tennis, they left the tennis courts. They went to Annie's house to chill. Because they were hungry, Annie thought it would be polite to give them something to eat. There was still a huge piece of the leg of roast left that her mother prepared for Sunday lunch. Her parents were still asleep and she thought her mother would not mind if she cut some of the meat for her friends. Anyway, she and her friends enjoyed the meal that she served with bread and coffee. By the time her parents woke up, they too were hungry and needed to eat. Annie and her friends were still sitting on the stoep at the front entrance. Annie was sitting the closest to the front door, and out of the door came her stepdad and he smacked her off from the garden chair. The blow was so fast and her two friends jumped up from their chairs all in shock of what happened.

'Glutton!' came the yell from his mouth. 'Today I will teach you a lesson, you little thief.'

'Sorry, Daddy.' Still protecting her face with her arm, she answered, not knowing what exactly she stole. There was no money or anything valuable in his car when she cleaned it earlier on. He went back into the house and came out with a big watermelon and a knife. The watermelon he put on the garden table and he started to cut it. He then gave her a big piece and instructed her to eat. She was still very full of the meat and bread they just had, but because she was scared to say no, she ate. The feeling of eating was not pleasant.

'Eat faster, you glutton, there is still a lot you must eat.'

'Daddy, I am full,' she said with a pleading trembling voice.

'You didn't think when you stole my meat.' When he said that, then she knew it was because of the meat she took. But this was her home and no one stole food from his or her own home and there was still such a lot of meat left on the roast pan. Still and all, she was so embarrassed because of this scenario playing out in the presence of her friends. They must hate her now because she gave them the food. Annie struggled with the second piece of watermelon, and from the corner of her eye, she saw her mother leaning against the wall. It was disturbing for her to see that her mother was just watching and said nothing about this humiliation. In her mind she prayed, wishing something serious would happen, like a hailstorm, just to stop this madness. Her stomach wanted to burst and she felt like vomiting. Her stepdad was watching her closely, cursing and asking questions. Then he proudly answered his own questions as if Annie was feeble-minded. She started to plead that she could not eat any more. Unfortunately the genuine-leather belt was used on her body and every stroke came down with violent anger. The contact of the belt on her body was painful and she wasn't sure which pain was worse. Was it the pain inflicted to cause bodily harm or was the emotional pain more severe, because she felt numb with both. It was between her screams, pain, and nausea, and her mother still said nothing.

Betrayal is what Annie feels although she sees the pain in her mother's eyes. Annie knows that it is forbidden for her mother to say anything because she too would get a blow in her face. Anyway, she thinks deeper and silently thinks that if she has children one day, this would never happen to them. She would rather take the blow than see her children getting it. Then again, her mother is who she is.

Her two now-bewildered friends stood like statues with their faces wet with their tears and confusion. They were scared and did not know what to say. Was the punishment not enough for this mean man to enjoy, or is he not pleased yet? Why does he not just slit her throat with the knife that's lying on the garden table? Annie felt desperate to just pass out and give up the ghost, but what about all her beautiful dreams? No, she would rather not die, not even now. Another blow of his hand struck the back of her head. The chewed watermelon gushed out of her mouth and she felt like fainting.

But, then came the mercy Annie thought of—the hailstorm. Tania's father was disrupted from his radio program by her screams. He came out from his house to investigate what was happening. He was so angry when he saw his neighbour with the belt in his hand and screamed at him to leave Annie alone. The vicious man was always careful of Tania's dad. The fact is, he was a woman beater but was scared of other men.

'Mr Jones, she stole meat and all I am doing is teaching her to ask instead of taking without permission". The so-called king said with much respect.

Shocked by what he just heard, Mr Jones sneered. 'Are you beating that child up for a piece of meat, how sick is that?'

'It was more than just a piece,' he replied.

'I don't care if it was a whole cow, you better put that belt down or I will call the cops.' The cruel man complied at once and went into the house. The two friends helped their friend up from the floor and cleared the table. Mr Jones went back into his house, and Annie's friends too had to leave because it was already late. Annie remained on the stoep, looking at the sun that was close to retiring for the day. The marks that the genuine-leather belt left on her body were still burning but she was more interested in the colourful flame of the sunset. Her eyes were focused on the melting rays of the sun, and deep in her heart, she knew the sun bore witness of this day. Then her mother, who called her for a big dose of castor oil, interrupted her moment. Her stepdad said nothing this time; he was too embarrassed because of the way his neighbour ostracized him. To Annie it was just another day of her history that was written before the foundation of time. Tomorrow she would get revenge by winning somebody's marbles. She always won. Last time Tony, a boy in the street, played with her and she won all his marbles. That night his mother came to complain and her stepdad gave her a hiding in front of Tony and she had to give all his marbles back. She promised herself never to play with him again because he was a sore loser and a mommy's boy. From that day, she could never eat watermelon again.

Nevertheless, months later, two ladies, Marie and Joan from the Kalahari, came to live with them. They found work in the city and had no place to stay at the time. Nellie offered them the room to share with Annie until they found a place of their own. Annie's bedroom now was changed, a single bed was fitted and a small wardrobe to cater for the clothes of the two ladies. Even though Annie was a bit sad because her desk and chair had to go, she was at least enjoying the company of Joan and Marie. They told her many stories about the Kalahari and life on their farm and promised to take her with them the next time they went.

Nellie thought now that they had boarders, her husband wouldn't fight too much, but that was not the case. Howbeit, Nellie was like a mother to her boarders and they would do Annie's hair and play with her. It was sad for these ladies to see what this woman Nellie with her beautiful heart and her daughter had to go through. Annie overheard them talking how they had to get out of this house because they were not used to such a lifestyle.

In the September school holidays of that year, the ladies took Annie with them to the farm in the Kalahari as they had promised. They travelled with the big van of their brother.

They travelled for many miles but eventually arrived at four in the morning at the farm. It was a normal time for farm people to be up. Joan and Marie's parents were so happy to see them. Their two younger sisters grabbed them with joy, and everyone asked questions about life in the big city of Johannesburg and couldn't stop talking. Annie was amazed to see so much love with firm hugs, and she couldn't stop watching what was playing out.

Happiness is truly a matter of choice, she thought, and could only wish that it could be like that with her family. Marie wanted Annie to go lie down to rest but Annie was too overwhelmed with excitement to be sent off to bed.

Marie's dad was complaining about a hungry cheetah that had already had a taste of his sheep. As a result, Annie couldn't help but listen with nervous attention to their conversation. According to Marie's dad, they had to spend money to fix the broken fence, and money is what should be respected because in the Kalahari it is scarce. Aunt Fila, the mother of the house, poked the coal stove and added more coal. Uncle Jake offered to help but Aunt Fila refused by saying, 'Son you drove for many hours and my curves need this exercise.' Everyone in the kitchen broke into a harmonious laugh. Annie was blown away to see how jolly with excitement this family was.

The whole family had coffee in the massive farm kitchen and Annie enjoyed listening to their conversation; she observed everything with intense concentration. Marie's dad told stories about the hunters who came from afar to hunt and the Bushman who knew all the plants and made medicines. The old man was very excited for his Coca-Cola his daughters brought for him. Annie watched as he paused to sip with so much appreciation and say this was the taste of the city. Joan teased her dad by saying it can never beat the fresh farm milk on an early morning. They all laughed about her gesture and she gave a big smile of approval. It is evident that all these little tales were priceless to Annie—it was like reading a book. She read the body language of everyone here. She strongly believed that this family who loved each other so dearly believed in strong family values. They didn't make war with each other and knew how to speak with respect to one another, no demeaning words and no cattishness.

At four thirty in the morning, already the heat of the big coal stove was at its peak. The two younger sisters started making breakfast for the family but were eager not to miss out on anything. Two farmworkers carried the boxes of groceries that we brought from the city and packed them out in the pantry. Marie and Joan were in deep conversation with their father about money matters, and his daughters listened to him with great respect. One could hear that the other workers were talking, merely outside preparing tools and donkey cars. It was a sign of a new working day. All this for Annie was so magnificent and her mind was running wild. To her this was like a story from a library book. They all enjoyed a big farm breakfast together and the travellers were not interested to go and rest, especially Annie. She was too happy to be in her element, and couldn't wait to venture into the bush veldt with this awesome family. Marie promised her that they would show her around to get the real feel of the bush veldt.

After the breakfast, Annie stood outside on the veranda that covered almost the whole house and she was watching the rising of the sun. Her frozen gaze fixed with immense attention as far as her eyes could see. The horizons were endless, and the red sandy savannah interacted with the colour of the rising sunbeams. The vast bone-dry plains boasted of a unique magical beauty and it was breathtaking. She understood what she saw and she cherished it as if it was her rightful place to be here in this moment in time.

The little girl becomes fearless now and locked in a moment of intense tranquillity. Was she in the mind of the Creator when he created all of this? Yes, she was because here she is to enjoy this moment with abundant appreciation for the beautiful creation. Her faculty of consciousness is taking pleasure in this intense and satisfying momentous event. The point is that it is the same sun she always sees in the city. But, it is so different here because the sun has a deep red, almost a rusty colour. The open space gives the horizon a glamorous appearance, and to her, it is a gift from nature. Birds gave praise by singing their morning tunes declaring that the Kalahari was awakening into a beautiful paradise—home of the Bushman. What indescribable beauty, she thought, and how different from the city life—this is what one may call a divine decree. Yet with all this beauty, the Kalahari too has its own dangers.

Her moment was interrupted by loud screams coming from the other side of the house, and she curiously ran to the direction where the noise came from. Everyone was standing around, and when Marie saw Annie, she signalled with her hand to come along.

'Come see, Annie, it's a two-meter-long mamba,' she said excitedly.

The now-excited Annie rushed forward to ease her curiosity. 'Are they going to kill it, Aunt Marie?' The little girl from the city asked.

'No, darling, Uncle Jake is going to release it back into the desert because it lost its way—look in the sack.' The little girl from the city peeped into the sack and gasped away. She loved many things about nature, but this big snake is way too much for her liking. Nevertheless, she is pleased that the snake will be returned to its own territory and not be killed.

Time out on this farm and being surrounded by so many loving people was what Annie needed. Such an adventurous holiday is what every child her age dreams of. Marie and Joan took her with them in the van every morning, when they milked the cows and collected wild cucumbers for salad. It was a special thing for her to eat home-made bread with home-made butter. Marie showed Annie how to mix the butter.

'It is a special skill, the secret is in the mixing method,' she said with much pride. Here on this farm, Annie learned so much, and it was nice to be away from the evil look of her stepdad. If only she could remain here, but she must go back to school.

Friday night all were invited to the neighbour's farm for a dance, and Joan and Marie took Annie with them on the donkey car. Annie could not believe that she was on a donkey car, and yes, it was a bumpy ride when the wheels of the donkey car clashed with humps on stones. The sun was starting to set and the Kalahari started to cool down. It was a long ride but it was fun.

At the party, which was held in a stable, her eyes peered as she watched the couples as they danced, but she was enjoying the braai and the ginger beer. A middle-aged man who happened to be the owner of the farm offered Annie dry wors and biltong. He was bragging about the spices he used for his special biltong. Annie cautiously asked him about the spices, but he only smiled and said it was a secret. She returned the smile and promised that she would enjoy it with great appreciation.

Later that night she retired from the adults, lying on her back with hand behind her head in the donkey car. It was the best view of the open night sky. Never had she seen the Milky Way so clearly exposed because there was no electricity. Here people only use oil lamps and candles or paraffin, and when they don't use their coal stoves, then they cook on a man-made fire outside. During that cooking process, the family enjoys talking about the day's activities. With much consideration, she was now convinced that too much harsh light does affect the dazzling glitter of the stars. Scattered and placid—such beauty to behold and yet life can be so complicated. But the time she spent with delightful people is a blessing for her because she is far away from her strict stepdad with his evil eyes and aggravation.

This is farm life, in the bush veldt—and life is different, poised and beautiful. However, the people here are hard-working and they don't waste water or anything, for that matter.

Annie was in total shock one morning when she saw Marie's father taking the hot kettle from the stove with his bare hand. Anyway, she had no intentions to question the fatherly man, with his handsome face and broad shoulders. She gathered that this was life in the Kalahari—people were not only brave, but also strong. As for their knowledge about medicines, every remedy came from the plants and the roots of the Kalahari. Yesterday a large thorn cut Joan on her hand while picking wild cucumbers, and her mother treated the cut with a leaf and olive oil. Today there was no sign of that cut. How amazing.

Here the cock crows to wake you up. At night one can hear the barking hyenas scavenging for their meals. Many animals can be heard warning fiercely with uproarious intimidation to those who dare to trample on their territory. Some nights, the owls sit on the roof of the house. It is a vast difference from life in the city, where one only hears the barking dogs and vehicle engines. As an example, out here at night all will sit on the veranda, enjoying small talk and coffee or listening to the news from the small portable radio. No television or electric appliances, even the handle of the kettle is a home-made contraption made out of the wire of a clothing hanger. Joan brought three house brooms because here they made one from the long grass they get in the veldt. Aunt Fila showed much appreciation for those brooms. As for the water, it does not run from taps, every third day it is taken from the borehole close to the stables. So when you are thirsty, you get water from the enamel bucket standing in the coolest spot in the kitchen, on a wooden table. Outdoor cold showers are a unique experience, but at night it is a bit risky because of the snakes. The water is kept in a tank on top of the shower and then you pull a chain that's hanging down. The water will then spray your body. Annie tried it once but she preferred to wash in the enamel dish. There is a way that you do it. First you wash your face and neck then the upper body. From there you sit in the dish and wash your private parts and bum. The last step, you stand in the dish and wash your feet and legs. Aunt Fila made her own soap but was delighted when Joan gave her a packet full of face soap she bought in the city.

Not to forget the long-drop toilet out in the yard, therefore at night a bucket is used for emergencies. Annie herself preferred to use the bucket.

They say the Kalahari can be harsh and unforgiving with its seasons. However, those who love it here survive victoriously and would never be happy in the big cities. The Kalahari is home to them, and without this habitat, they would feel banished; they are destined to be here. The essence and the moments of wonder here can only be appreciated when one has experienced the heartbeat of the Kalahari with its remarkable beauty and mysteries. Annie believes that her time here will be a new page in the history of her life. It is a break she will never forget. Only time will tell if she would ever return to the beautiful Kalahari in the future.

However, like all good things must come to an end, so Annie's ten-day September break also came to its end. Moreover, it was one she would never forget. In addition, the stories she would be able to share at school about her stay in the Kalahari would make headlines to her classmates. This was an unusual experience because not many kids had a school break in the Kalahari with its rust sand dunes. Somehow the oxygen of the Kalahari had sanitized the mind of Annie, but now she had to go back to her reality in the house of pain.

Later the next year, Marie and Joan found a two-bedroom accommodation and moved out. They promised that they would visit on weekends and sometimes sleep over. Life went back to the same way again, and her desk and chair were back in her room.

# CHAPTER 4

There are many scenarios that Annie can recall, painful ones, and yet sometimes her stepdad showed his human qualities too. Generally speaking, it brought more confusion to Annie's mind. He would call her and tell her she is going to get new clothes and one day he even surprised her with a beautiful red bicycle. This red bicycle he bought in Lenasia. However, she was always alert because he always had unsavoury motives behind his good deeds, when it came to her. Maybe he was planning to kill her and then he would testify in court and show the new bicycle saying, 'Why will I waste my money knowing that I am going to kill her?' A good alibi, Annie thought—then she heard him proudly say, 'Now you can cycle to school instead of walking,' with a smile. She was shocked and scared at the same time. All she could think of was that her mother spoke some sense into his head. Accepting the good deed, she dismissed the negative thinking from her mind. Notwithstanding, for once she was a happy child for that day. If only he could be like this forever until she was grown up and be away from him. Other than all the problems, she enjoyed having a bicycle of her own.

Months went by and each day came with its new dynamics. The king fights with his wife and stepdaughter, and then Nellie takes her child and leaves the house to move in with her mother Delia. After they were away from home for a week or two, then he would go knock on his mother-in-law's door with new promises of how he had changed and his wife would take the bait and go back home. The cycle goes on and on as many months and even years go by. In the meantime, Annie grows into a beautiful young girl. She excels in school and is still active in sports. However, like any other teenager, she also becomes rebellious and gives backchat to her mother when the king is not around.

One day, her mother sent her to the shop for tomatoes because she was already late with the cooking and wanted to fix a quick meal before the king came from work. She met a friend at the shop and the two of them got lost in a lengthy chat. By the time she got home with potatoes instead of tomatoes, her mother chased her and threw the potatoes at her. Unfortunately some of the kids saw and laughed out loud. Annie was furious and started chasing the kids, throwing at them the potatoes her mother threw at her. When she got into the house, she was given a hiding with a slipper but that made her angrier, and for the first time, she had an outburst against her mother.

'Why don't you hit your ugly man with your slipper? Is it not enough that you stand like a statue when he hits me with his belt?' Nellie was in total shock but she had no time to argue; she had to prepare the king's meal. Annie went to her room to think and realized that the effects of emotional abuse from her stepdad were starting to change her personality. She felt bad about her behaviour towards her mother because they were both victims of their abuser. It was distressing for her to think that she had trampled on her mother's heart with such demeaning words.

Sometimes she hates her mother for accepting this life but now she feels sad and doesn't know how to overcome this feeling. It is evident that emotional abuse can make it hard for the victim to say sorry. Annie is not comfortable with saying sorry. She sees how the king degrades, insults, and makes her mother look stupid in the presence of others. Her mother is afraid of him and so is she. So, later or tomorrow, when things are more settled, then she will try to say sorry to her mother for crossing the line.

Nonetheless, they are like any other family; they go on holidays, camping trips, and visits to his friends or family. December holidays the king would sometimes take them to his family in the Cape Province, but most of his family makes all kinds of excuses why they cannot host them.

They would then either end up in a tent at a camping area on the beach or his mother is forced to open her door. It does not come as a surprise because honestly no one likes her stepdad, not even his own family. Being among his family gave him more rope to perform with Nellie and Annie. He was under the impression that the family sees his action as brave and honourable, but they were not at all impressed. They too had seen him as mean and evil especially if he cursed their children. Annie couldn't help but wonder if his family would ever attend his funeral one day because they don't make it a hidden secret that they don't appreciate his presence. He even interfered in the people's religion, and his sister gave him a warning about it by saying, 'One day you are going to find someone that will stand up against you and you will get the hiding of your life from that person. We only say nothing because we respect you.'

The king did not waste time, protecting his honour by answering, 'I still have to meet the one who can beat me up.' Annie had the urge to laugh because she knew he could only hit females but so did his family because when he said that; some of the youngsters forced out coughs in a very sarcastic way. Annie could only imagine that it was a sign of silently calling him a useless woman-beater. His sister's husband was not impressed with his words saying their religion would take them all to hell. He walked out of the kitchen, mumbling that it was better for him to walk away from this ignorant man because he would only smash his face. The king said nothing in defence, but how could he because his brother-in-law was a well-built man with a fast fist. The amused bewilderment of the youngsters showed great disappointment for the absence of a fight. On the other hand, Annie could also admit seeing him getting a good few kicks would have been the highlight of this holiday. The reason why Annie felt strongly that he needed a good spanking is that a few days earlier when she and the family children were all playing on the beach, the king made it his duty to come and give Annie a hiding on the beach with his belt. The reason being, she forgot to wash his car. If it weren't for the three surfers on the beach who came to Annie's rescue, then he would have really messed up Annie's face because that genuine-leather belt had no sense of direction. So yes, if Uncle Cee could have given him a punch on the nose, it was going to be okay in Annie's eyes.

Anyway, a few days later, they left for Johannesburg because the king shortened the holiday, complaining that he did not feel welcome or properly respected by his family. No one tried begging him to stay on for the complete duration of the holiday. It was quite clear that everyone welcomed his decision to go.

Back at home in Johannesburg, Annie is on her same old pattern again. The monotony she has grown accustomed to. She goes alone to church like she used to since she was small. Then there are still the questions from the king when she returns from church. She must know the scripture that was read from and has to elaborate on the sermon. Sometimes it gave Annie great joy to lie to him about these sermons, silently feeling that she is making a fool of him. Which in fact serves him right, because why does he not go to church if he is so eager to know what was preached?

Be that as it may, the routine of her stepdad is still the same, but being a teenager now, she copes much better with his ways. However, the one thing she cannot stand is when he embarrasses her in front of other people.

Now that she is in high school, she knows the time is slowly getting near for them to move on to the next level. As usual, she made new friends. Her friends loved her to bits, especially Judith and Bernadette. These two girls are very special to Annie. After school, they go with Annie and chill on the stoep together in the afternoons. Sometimes they help Annie to finish her chores. However, on that stoep many emotions are spilled. Annie listens patiently to the two girls she has so much love for. Meanwhile, they do not know that Annie too is in the same situation. But Annie has no plans to ever tell them; instead she is the advisor and the motivator. Together they cry and laugh and dream about their great future that is awaiting the three of them. Like Annie, these two girls go through a lot of verbal, emotional, physical, and mental abuse. Annie can relate to their emotional pain. There is a similar background and numerous other peculiarities. For her, it is imperative to remind her two friends that brighter days will come.

Nevertheless, there are so many things she is not allowed to do. She is not allowed to go to school camps or sleep over at a friend's house. She is not even allowed to visit her grandma, but that she secretly does when the king goes to work on certain Saturdays. In essence, all the things she is not allowed to do, do not disturb Annie Anonyma. For she knows there are too many things that she can do that other girls her age can't. She knows how to change the van's wheels, change the old car oil from the sump and replace it with new oil. For one thing, she can even remove the battery to clean the excess acid. There is no boy in their home, so since the age of seven, she was the one to make the fire in the coal stove. Before they had electricity, she was already using the primer stove to make tea for her parents. She knows how to use all the building and mechanical tools and can drive a motor vehicle. Can other girls her age drive and do they know how to use the tools and spanners? Yes, they cook and clean but so does she.

Not forgetting, her best secret skill is that she knows how to communicate with nature. In particular, she sings in the choir and singing is like writing. You share emotions and deep feelings. So all the chores her stepdad gives her to do as punishment and spite are what mould her and give her skills. Looking after her own veggie and flower gardens is not punishment to her. No, because nature is what she loves and it is made out of the same thing as her—energy. She feels that warmth when she hugs her tree. Nature connects with her and it motivates her to carry on because nature and Annie have a special relationship. The now full-grown peach tree is what she planted, and she loves that tree that gives the sweetest yellow cling peaches in season. Importantly, she speaks to her tree about her fears and her future plans. In turn, that tree does not judge her, no, that tree is patient and kind to her. She reads her library books under the grape tree because when it was but a little vine she nurtured and groomed that vine with her own hands. The fact of the matter is she has all the right to speak to her trees, because she loves them. They sense the vibrations of fear in her voice when she whispers. Can other youngsters listen to the wind when it blows, when she understands the language of the wind and knows when it is angry? They fear the lightning and she sees it as a report of anger from the universe.

On the other hand, polishing her stepdad's shoes and mowing the lawn is not a big deal for Annie. One day she might do it for her husband whom she will love. On that lawn she lies on her back and looks at the beautiful sky to gape at the clouds. The clouds move around and change into different images that remind her that her dreams of tomorrow are limitless. As for those roses that she prunes, they give off a fragrance that is pleasing to her nose, a beauty that makes her understands the perfume of nature.

Everything she has to do has a purpose. Her peers will see all of this as crazy but she lives in the real world. To Annie, the real world is about rules, time frames, terms and conditions, and last but not least, responsibility.

With all this considered, she does not see herself as abnormal because she thinks the same as other girls her age. When she is with them at school, she relates to them. They talk about boys and also discuss the human anatomy. She too explores with make-up and nice clothes. She is good-looking and greatly admired by the opposite sex. Her friends love her to bits, and her teachers appreciate her good manners. So what can be seen as abnormal about her? Of course she does admire the lives of other youngsters and the way they are spoiled. Be that as it may, there is no point in harbouring self-pity. One day she will spoil her own children and work hard to give them the lives she never had. Life is teaching her to press on, and believing in the power of God gives her hope and faith. She believes that her faith and hope will keep all the good memories alive. As for the king, he can never take her hope away.

# CHAPTER 5

Life at home is becoming more and more difficult. Because Annie is in high school and she has more homework and school projects. It is so hard for her to cope with chores and her schoolwork. It is so much that she even has to cut down on her reading. It is all becoming stressful and it all breaks down her self-esteem because now the king has given her another chore. In the afternoons, she has to sell vegetables on the corner and the other youngsters tease her, although the teasing is not the problem. The problem is that all these veggies must be packed in little plastic bags, and that takes so much time. It is much easier for the housewives to buy from Annie's stall because then they don't have to walk to the shop. Therefore she had enough customers, and when the king counts the takings at night, he is more than happy. At least he tells her now and then that one day she will make a good businessperson. Getting a compliment from him is like expecting donations from. The king says he is teaching Annie to become an entrepreneur, making it quite clear that he has no money to help her with further studies in the future. She has no problem with that, but she managed to make a deal with her mom. While she is at school, her mom makes up the packets, ready for her to sell. However, there are still the gardens, the lawn, the shoes, and her homework. Then she came up with an excellent plan: instead of selling from the corner, she decides to sell from the gate. So she tells all her customers that she will be selling from the gate at home. Aunty Daisy, who admires the perseverance of Annie, wanted to know why, and Annie told her about the other chores and her homework.

'Oh, my baby, one day all this will be over.' Some people from the neighbourhood knew quite well about Annie's stepfather and his abusive manner. Many times, Nellie got a few punches from him in the street and people looked on.

'Aunty Daisy, I will kill two birds with one stone. While waiting for a customer, I can hose the lawn and the flower beds. His safety and gumboots I can clean right at the gate, and when I'm done with that, I can at least do my homework on the chair. It will save me so much time,' Annie explained to the lady.

'It makes a lot of sense, child, I like the way you think.' She smiled at Annie with so much warmth.

'Thank you for understanding, Aunty Daisy, I know my stand was opposite your gate and now you have to walk to mine to buy,' Annie answered and returned the smile. The plan of action made her life much easier, and she even had time to read right at her stall. Tania helped Annie to sell and they took turns to go to the toilet. Tania liked to pass on the items and give the customers their change. Tania was very good with counting the money. Story time was never better for Tania, and Annie liked to read to her, right there at the gate.

Now the king sees the money and becomes greedy. He now sends one of the drivers from work on a Wednesday to buy fruit from the market. More work for Annie. He shouts at her because the fruit is not such a good sell, but how does that become Annie's fault? Tania, Andy, and Annie eat some of the fruit because the king does not count it. Life goes on and so does the business. Saturdays and Sundays, Annie does not sell because on Fridays most people get paid then they buy from the bigger shops. Every second Saturday, Annie goes to the library in town to exchange books. Sometimes she would go with her two friends down the road to play tennis.

One beautiful sunny Saturday, Annie and her two friends went to the tennis courts. The day was good and she was hitting the tennis ball to release all the stress and tension of the week, not merely knowing what is awaiting her at home. By the time she got home, the king was already back from work and as drunk as a lord. He was cursing and performing. Annie was nervous and scared. She walked nervously into the house, and when he saw her, he immediately started cursing her. 'Where the hell do you think you are coming from, little swine?'

Still standing with the tennis racket in her hand, Annie explains that she was at the tennis court. He gets up from the chair and smacks her not only once but twice in the face.

'You think life is about playing tennis,' he screamed at the now-bewildered Annie. He grabbed the tennis racket out of her hand, lifted his right leg, and broke the racket in half on his upper leg. Then he held it like a knife, aiming for her face, but his wife saw and jumped in the middle.

'You are not going to hit my child with that broken racket,' his wife blustered out. Surprised by the reaction of his wife, he started stabbing her with the broken racket. She blocked the blows with her arms to protect her daughter's face, and every time, the broken racket leaves a slashed wound. Blood came gushing out of the open flesh from Nellie's upper arms. The sharp pieces of wood that were stabbed into her upper arms left pieces of splintered wood behind. The more she tried to block the blows to her arms, the more he stabbed. Annie was standing behind her. She screamed viciously until he stopped. The blood was streaming down the arms of Nellie. Annie was hurt because those blows were meant for her but instead her mother took the punches. However, somehow Annie felt good that her mother stood up to defend her. Crossing the line is one thing, but stepping onto the parameters is another and the king was stepping on Nellie's parameter. Needless to say, Annie had seen what she always wanted to see—for her mother to stand up for her although the circumstances were as they were. Bamboozled, she stared in shock but looked at her mother as a heroine. That is to say, she had seen another side of her mother she had never seen before.

Anyway, she helped her mother by cleaning her wounds with pure alcohol and Savlon. She helped her mom by removing the splinters of the broken wood, put some antiseptic ointment on, and plastered the wounds to stop the blood. After a while the blood stopped oozing out. In the meantime the king just carried on cursing and drinking his beer and complained of being a victim in his own house.

Anyhow, life in the apartheid regime was tough and people lived from hand to mouth with the wages they were paid. The whole incidence was because the king found a small notebook in Annie's room with the names of the clients she gave credit for the vegetables and fruit they bought from her. Why was it such a bad thing because they all paid on Mondays? Why was he so mean and inhuman? Now her mother was in so much pain because he was nothing but a glutton for money, and selfish.

Later that night, her mom had a fever and was in great pain. Annie took painkillers from the medicine cabinet and gave them to her mom. By Monday, Nellie had to go to the doctor because the wounds were inflamed. Annie skipped school to accompany her mother. Each of the holes had two stitches, and when Annie looked at the wounds, her tears wanted to fall because her stepdad was aiming to damage her face. Her mother was a human shield who protected the face of her daughter from gruesome scars. Again she could not help but see the beauty in the ugliness. All things considered, she now knows that somehow her mother does love her. It can only be the love of a mother that would do such a brave deed for her child.

# CHAPTER 6

That day, after the visit to the doctor, Nellie got a restraining order against her husband. Then, she and Annie went to live with her mother and brother. During the day, Grandma and Uncle went to work. Annie went to school, and her mom cleaned up and cooked. On Sundays, Annie went to church with Grandma. Nellie refused to go, always worried that people would know that she left her husband. All the same, life is much better now.

One Saturday afternoon, Annie watched with great interest how her granny was starching the doilies. When the starch was dry, Granny ironed it with the medium-hot iron on the ironing board. When it was done, the doilies were no longer looking like a flat napkin. They had curves that formed some sort of wall and looked beautiful, and on Granny's face, there is a satisfied look of a job well done. Then Annie asked the random question to make conversation.

'How long have you been doing this, Mama?'

'Oh my, baby, long before you were born. I was working for a Jewish woman and had to do this a lot for the Pesah. Do you know what Pesah is?'

'It is when the Jews commemorate when they were set free as slaves from Egypt,' Annie answered enthusiastically.

'You are clever, where did you learn that from?'

'I am a reader, Mama, I like to read many books on history and cultures.'

'Yes, my child, reading provides information . . . do you know that the Jewish woman I worked for named you.' Now Annie was surprised and very inquisitive.

'Really, Mama, and why was that, because I don't have a Jewish name.' Granny smiled and shook her head in slow motions.

'My child, life can be full of many surprises. When your mother was pregnant with you, we were very poor and your uncles were still at school. Your grandpa was working for the railway . . . but let me tell you how you got your name. I was doing what I was doing now, ironing the doilies for my Jewish boss but I was very sad that day.'

'Why were you sad, Mama?'

'My child, I was so sad because you had to be born anytime from that day and I was worried because we were unprepared.'

'Unprepared for my birth, Mama?' Annie said with great disappointment.

'No, baby, unprepared because we had nothing for you. No clothes and not even a nappy pin. Anyway, the Jewish lady saw the worry on my face, and what do you think happened next?' Granny asked.

'You had to tell her about all your concerns, Mama.'

'Yes, and I did.' Granny asked Annie to pass the other doilies, and with a lack of impatience, she quickly passed another set. Granny took her time to lay them out on the ironing board, and Annie's impatience was now getting a hold of her nerves.

'I am still listening, Mama.'

'Wait, child, I must put them in a straight line so that I can iron them perfectly.' Annie waited with anticipation but still Granny took her time. Eventually when Granny was satisfied with the way she spread each doily apart from another, she talked.

'Now where was I?'

'Where you told her about all your concerns, Mama.'

'Yes, after listening to me, my Jewish boss said nothing and left me in the laundry. After an hour she called me to the bedroom and I was surprised to see her dressed in white and every piece of furniture was covered with white sheets. I was confused and worried if I maybe did something wrong, but then she told me that she had laid my petition before God. She handed me a notepad and a pen and asked me to write down everything the baby was going to need. She insisted that I should leave nothing out.' Annie was so eager to hear what happened next, and it was as if her granny was to slow to continue the conversation.

'So was it some kind of ritual, Mama?' Annie asked.

'No, my child, she was praying about it, asking God to direct her what to do.'

'So did you write down the list?'

'I did.' Granny sighed and looked up for a moment to observe her granddaughter's face then she continued with the story.

'I gave her the list then she asked me for a cup of tea. I went to the kitchen to make the tea but I could hear her speaking on the phone in her own language. By the time I took the tea to her, she handed me a piece of paper,' Granny continued.

'What was on the paper?' Annie asked with anxious curiosity.

Granny again looked up to Annie and said, 'An address of a Jewish shop for me to collect every item I wrote on that list.' Annie's mouth was open with the shock of excitement now running through her body, and Granny nodded.

'I told her that I will never be able to pay her back, but she said it was paid in full, then the lady went on, saying, 'All you need to do is to give the child the name I give you because the child will be special and the child will take after the meaning of the name. But when the child reaches the age of fifty, the child must be given the Star of David to carry around the neck as a symbol of jubilee.' Annie laughed bashfully and said, 'I am very far from fifty, Mama.'

Granny smiled back at her and answered, 'Now you know how special you are, whatever happens in your future only God knows. So go make your granny a nice cup of tea in the queen's cup.'

Happy with the way her granny always talks to her, she thinks of the different tone her stepdad would use. The voice of the man with the polluted mind is always commanding and authoritative. He navigates what he wants, blustering as if he owns the whole universe, and his presence would bring an uneasy feeling to any human being. He is a ruthless man with a cold facial expression. Pondering on the thoughts of him sends down a cold quiver down her spine. In an instant, she changes her thinking to another direction to secure the beauty of her grandmother's words.

Who would ever give her the Star of David? No one of her family is Jewish, or is this just one of Granny's tales trying to make her happy? If so, then it works because in this moment she is happy.

Being in the house of her gran, she feels safe and secure and she enjoys the vocabulary her gran so often uses to emphasize what she tries to bring across. It was a sentence that would say, '*Nobody can tell me how many beans can make six.*' In proper English it means, you can't teach me what I already know. The phrase Annie really likes is '*I don't even have a coin to scratch behind my ear*'—it means, I am broke.

Life is all gloomy, until . . . Yes, until one day, the king turns up with presents and a bunch of flowers and many promises of how he has changed and is no longer drinking. Annie asks her mother if she could rather stay with her uncle and grandmother but her mother refused. Together with her mother she goes back to the situation—back to the *unpredictable house of pain*. Grandma and Uncle seem to understand but why can't they explain it to Annie because maybe she too will understand. Back into the home of her stepdad again away from the secure haven of her grandmother's house, the invisible mask will have to go back onto her face—it is her disguise. Again she will have to release the power to persevere. Needless to say, one day the puzzle will be complete but for now she has to be content with herself.

As the days went by, Annie started craving for a life of peace, harmony, and love. For one, it is only normal to feel that way because she is a human being. Although all went well for some time, it was barely a fortnight then the old tricks of the king come to the fore. The insults and the physical abuse were worse this time. Subsequently, it was as if he wanted to pay revenge because they left the last time. Weekends were the worse because his excessive drinking made him madder, then Annie and her mom were subjected to his physical abuse. Not that she expected life to be rosy—she knew soon it would happen again. For one thing, he had a regime and not her or Nellie can destabilize his regime. However, his dictatorship will come to an end because Annie will not remain a child. That is a road map imprinted in her mind, and his annoying voice will be silent. If she holds on to sound mind, she will persevere until the day this vermin will be eradicated for good. Annie sits and analyzes many things.

There is a danger that adults don't take note of. Never ill-treat a child and think that he or she will forget about it because they were too young. Children remember, and they can become damaged in such a way that they will come back for you when they are grown up. Life has a cycle; when you are a baby, you are frail and need tender care. Furthermore, as that baby grows up, you as the adult grow older and can become frail. Then the old person too needs to be looked after. So now the cycle changes. We need to take care of and love our children because when we are old, then our children need to take care of us. It is the cycle but will Annie with the invisible mask really care for this man when he is old? 'Hell no!' she thought and really felt like laughing out loud. She would rather care for a wild animal but as for this man it is a big no, no.

Having this debate with herself makes her to think more profoundly. Did she maybe water the seed of hatred, is she nurturing revenge, knowing that revenge is a common passion but can change the sane mind into a lethal weapon?

Then she visualizes when she was younger. She sees herself standing on the little bench to get to the primer stove, her shaking hand pouring the paraffin through the funnel into the tummy of the primer. Then when the task is completed she pumps the primer and lights it up with the matches. The flame is ready, and the teapot with water she places on top of the primer stove. While she waits for the water to boil, she prepares the two cups and matching saucers in the tray. When the water reaches boiling point, she removes the teapot and puts the smaller milk pot on the flame to warm up. Now the tea leaves go into the teapot; she stirs the tea with a teaspoon to get it strong. Once this mixture is strong enough, the milk warm, then she switches the primer stove off and pours the tea and warm milk into the cups, and off Cinderella would go to serve the morning tea on a tray together with the sugar bowl. It was her first duty on weekends and public holidays. With a smile on her face, she says to herself, 'I could do what other girls my age couldn't do.' She loved that primer stove because it was her little stove. She sang when she cleaned the brass body of that stove with Brasso polish. In the same way, she polished her stoep with the Sunbeam polish once a week. On that stoep, she had many conversations with the sun and the moving clouds; the sky was never unfriendly to her. They know her pain, and there were many times when that stoep floor caught her tears of despair and quiet moments. The greatest times on the stoep were with Judith and Bernadette. They would talk endlessly about many things, laugh and daydream about their future.

After all, even her bedroom knows her feelings. She loves nature but nature can also show its anger and it can be scary. Annie had experienced some of those moments. One stormy night, she was lying quietly in her bed, listening to the angry cry of the wind. A storm was angrily voicing its opinion, and the thunder answered with violent aggression. Annie continued to remain quiet and scared but at the same time she tried to figure out everything, not sure what this outburst was about. To Annie it was as if the atmospheric forces were having a massive dispute and, without anyone's approval, showed their insubordination. Every minute the wind would answer with a rough defiance, and it was not long when the rain came down in a hurried rush. The onslaught was in action. Annie could only imagine that all the stars did not want to get involved. Therefore, they kept out of this by not even revealing themselves from the dark, angry but patient sky that was accustomed to this kind of contention. Annie felt scared and alone in the dark cold bedroom and she wished Tania could be with her. She wished her mother could come into her room for a moment to check on her, but also knew that it was not about to happen. As a child she had trained her mind not to depend on the sympathy of others, but for now she is in dire need of a pair of arms to hug her. Nevertheless, to shield herself from the flashes of the lighting, she slowly pulled the blanket to cover her face and eyes. The storm outside was blasting with domineering fury. This ongoing argument was uproarious. Annie was frightened and worried about her plants and yellow cling peach tree. She felt guilty that she was terrified because she regarded herself as brave—but then she turned her focus to the Bible on the day when Jesus was at sea with his disciples. They too were scared of the storm that night, and yet they were holy men. She then decided to think that this process of her fear was human.

With her face still under the blanket, she wished the argument could settle. Then at least her heart would return to its normal beats. Meanwhile, nothing goes on forever, and even this raging storm ended its anger and the night turned silent. It wasn't long for Annie to peacefully slip off to dreamland.

Those are the little scenarios Annie can recall and smile about.

# CHAPTER 7

Life is not easy and each day it becomes more and more complex but life must go on. Annie had a secret she kept from everyone. Mrs Kwan from the Chinese shop saw the marks on Annie's mom's arms and asked Annie about it. Because the lady defended Annie before, she felt compelled to tell her the truth. From the next day, Mrs Kwan has secretly trained Annie in kung fu—the art of self-defence. Mrs Kwan imprinted in Annie's mind that self-defence is not murder. To begin with, Annie trained hard and meditated the way she learned from Mrs Kwan. As her training progressed, she then trained with nunchaku, the sword, and knives. Mrs Kwan was proud of her student that trained so fiercely, and Annie just loved her traditional gear from China. Being dressed in her gi always gave her a feeling of confidence and self-respect. The sensei forbade Annie to train in other clothes. So

Annie was toned and did a lot of the breathing exercises and meditation. To Annie, her sensei was strict, wise, and very strong for her age. She had many techniques she used, always saying it's because she was so short. Annie's favourite weapon in her art of kung fu was the nunchaku, which she mastered with excellence.

One day she asked her sensei a question.

'Mrs Kwan, why are some people so fortunate and others are not?'

'The cause of events cannot always be predicted, we all get to taste the bitter, the salty, the sour, and the sweet. Sometimes one grows up in a family that loves you and protects you, and then the course of your life can suddenly change by a wrong choice. You get married to someone and become a slave of abuse. It can happen with love, business, addictions, and many other facets but we can never predict our own future.' The sensei explained with a genuine expression of deep concern on her face.

'How can we prevent it?' Annie asked with an inquiring mind.

'You can't because you don't know when it will strike,' came the answer.

'Is there a way one can prepare for the unfortunate event . . . maybe?'

'That is why you train in self-defence, because it helps you to be disciplined, and right now you are a student of your own history.'

'Is that all to it, because I sometimes feel that I am nurturing the bad seed inside of me and I don't want to hate those who wrong me.'

'No, there are many other ways, and one vital process is to be empowered with education because no one can take that away from you. So you better learn hard in school—but water the seed closer to your heart.'

'I am struggling a bit, Mrs Kwan, I just make it and my marks are always just average, and because I now water the wrong seed, my mind is troubled and I can't concentrate.'

'Going through what you do, it is understandable, that is why you must free the darkness from your mind by meditating and you will see the world in all its glory because then in no uncertain terms we expel the coarse, the bitter, and the sour. Nothing will then contaminate the beauty of your spirit. Don't always prepare for the worst, there is sometime some beauty even in the ugly, and that beauty in the ugly is what maybe one day will refine you as a human. When one's mind is clear, one does not look for truth, truth will find you.'

'Life is an uncertain sound, Mrs Kwan.'

'But life is a gift and it teaches us many different skills. Life can be kind and unkind, but you should treasure it with your heart and learn to be tolerant. You taste the bitter and the sour now and it is unappetizing and hard to swallow but one day you will also taste the sweet—then after tasting honey, you will never eat golden syrup again. You will know how to be the captain of your own ship.' As Mrs Kwan slowly walked away from Annie, she looked back and said, 'The wheel of life keeps on turning, clean the battle in your mind.' Annie was satisfied with what she heard from her wise sensei.

Every day she pondered on that honey she will one day taste and how she will steer her own ship because she will be the captain. She thought of looking for a book about ships, with her next visit to the library. It will be nice to know about all the dynamics of ships and the duty of a captain. As for the wheel of life, she wished she could help it to turn a little faster. Mrs Kwan had planted a seed in her head and she needed to feed that seed to see the outcome of its growth. Just like with her grapevine, peach tree, and gardens—there is always an outcome and it is called results. It is possible that superior elements can be found in anything.

# CHAPTER 8

As time goes by, Annie's personality grows more and more vivaciously. The kung-fu training is good for her because it builds the capacity of her endurance. She tries hard to guard against the hatred she feels. For one thing, the unfriendly looks on her stepfather's face are no longer threatening her. Besides, she will be the captain of her own ship one day and fear will cease to exist in her life. For this reason, the proper order will be restored. His criticism has no effect on her because now she knows there is good even in the ugly and maybe the ugly will refine her as a human. She will measure up to all the standards that she will set for herself, and that will be the benefit of her expertise. All that matters now is that the wheel of life is turning slowly, and her pot of honey is waiting for her to taste.

She often thinks of the Star of David she is going to get on her fiftieth birthday one day because it will be her jubilee. However, she is not sure who would give it; she wished she knew but trusted that it will happen. Granny was so serious that day when she told her, and there were tears in her eyes, therefore she believed the story of that star. Maybe one day this whole puzzle of her complicated life will fall into place and be complete. That is what she will call the fate of her jubilee.

Years later:

One day while playing tennis on the courts, she sees a young guy about the same age as her. She likes what she sees and tries hard to get his attention. Her friends notice and tell her to go talk to him but she refuses because she knows a guy should be the hunter.

'But how is he going to know that you like him if you don't talk to him?' her friend says with a playful smile.

'Fate and time,' she answers.

'In the meantime somebody else might spot him.' The friend was teasing her.

'If it is meant for us to be together, then it will be so but one thing I can tell you is that I will get married to him one day.'

'You really do like him that much.'

'I am serious.'

This is how the sequence went for many months in Annie's life. She was always on the tennis court to see her future husband. Many times she made eye contact with him and smiled with her angelic smile that usually brightened up any situation. One day she invited her class friends to accompany her to the stadium because her future husband's school had their sports day and he was one of the athletes. Her friends were eager to see the young man they heard so much about during lunch breaks at school. Then again she made the statement when he was on the field, showing her friends a proud face.

'Look! There he is, my husband-to-be.' To the friends it was a joke, but one girl agreed with Annie that nothing is impossible. The others were jesting that she didn't even know his name but had the guts to make such statements. It was all such a big joke, but those were the words that drove Annie to the limits. In the same month, she knew his name and his telephone number. The next year, they had a go-slow relationship because he was younger than her. They kissed a few times and phoned one another endlessly. Many girls were envious when they see them holding hands on the tennis courts or at the school's sports day in the stadium. Annie was very happy because she was in love. Then one day there was a change in the situation. The vicious husband had again beaten Nellie so badly that she finally made up her mind to leave with her child for good. Leaving for good was not the problem; the problem was leaving Johannesburg to go and live in the Eastern Cape. This was devastating news for Annie because now she had to leave her boyfriend behind. Her boyfriend knew about the situation and always promised Annie that one day he would take her away from the abusive life. Annie believed him because he loved her and she knew it. The day of departure, she and her boyfriend made a promise to stay true to each other, and Annie promised him that she would return.

Six months later, a family member managed to put Annie in a new school. She made new friends and had long telephone conversations with her boyfriend in Johannesburg. They missed each other profusely. Nellie found a job to look after a young married couple's child and the household. Weekends, Annie visited Nellie in the suburb where she worked. Everything seemed fine and life went on as normal. However, normal changes but to no surprise for Annie—because months later, the king rocks up unannounced. He does the same trick and Nellie goes back to Johannesburg with him. This time Annie had to stay behind because she had to finish the school year. She was left with family and realized that her mother only loved her stepfather and not her. She now knew what she would do at the end of the year. She would go back to Johannesburg and go live with her grandmother and uncle. From now on, her mother may go on with her own life but without her. Now that she lives with family, life is much better for her. At least she can hang around with school friends and cousins. Some Saturdays they go to the beach or visit other family members and friends. Some Fridays or Saturdays they go to the nightclub and dance the night away.

Life with her stepdad was different; all she had to do was to abide by his rules, shouts, and abuse. Chores were what she even had living with her family, but you did your work and when you were done, the day was yours—especially weekends. No one fought, cursed, or ill-treated her here. Here in her aunt's house she was at home because the house was a home and not ruled by a governing body. One became disciplined and was scolded if one stepped out of line but it was done in a civilized way and with love. As for her school friends, they were free to visit her.

Thinking and weighing all the sad belittling and humiliating moments takes her mind back to a Saturday when she had school friends who popped in without notifying her. That was one hectic embarrassing day she never wanted to experience again. The two school friends greeted the king, and he rudely told them to leave without even greeting them back. They tried to explain that they came to visit Annie, but he cursed them. As they were leaving he let loose the dog to chase them. They screamed as they were running for the gate. To the king it was a big joke, and as for Annie, she did not know where to put her head the way she was embarrassed by the nasty deed.

Nevertheless, she knew that on Monday the whole school would know about the saga.

The Monday at school when the girls asked Annie about it, she gave them a weird story about an uncle who was mentally ill. She apologized, and the whole incidence was thrown into the box of forgetfulness. She was always very good to explain many embarrassing incidents because it was a mechanism she used to protect her from slandering tongues. She would never tell anybody that the king was her stepdad because then they would feel sorry for her. It was only her sensei and the friends down the road who knew. Not even Tania was aware of it. It was enough that she felt sorry for the situation she was in, and she did not need others to do that on her behalf. Besides, freedom and a beautiful life were awaiting her. So going back to her mother and stepdad she would never even consider again. The one thing that made her happy right now was that she was going to see her boyfriend, whom she loved so much. The man she picked on the tennis court to marry her someday and her course would be altered.

# CHAPTER 9

The school year was over, and Nellie sent money to Annie to travel by train back to Johannesburg. Annie did not wait for the matric ball because she was dreaming to see the love of her life again. She travelled back to Johannesburg and from town she took a taxi to her grandmother's place. Her mother questioned her about her decision, and she begged her mother to allow her to stay with her uncle and grandmother.

Annie did not apply for a bursary to go study further and decided to look for a job. She browsed through all the newspapers in the job-finding section. Her gran and uncle gave her money to go into town every day to go job hunting. It was the norm then—all students would go to companies to inquire about a job. She even tried the library but they too had no open positions. Many places needed people who had more qualifications and work experience, which she did not have. The situation broke down Annie's self-esteem, especially now that she felt free and ready to embark on a new journey. Her hope for her new life was fractured, and she was scared that it would get infected. For many months it went on like this. Granny even put in a prayer request in church for the congregation to pray for Annie to find a job. Her boyfriend saw her anxiety to find a job and told her to take things easy because everything has its own time. He reminded her of her extraordinary gifted mind and told her all would be fine. However, all this was causing tremendous delays for her to make something of her life, because the king once said she would never do anything worthwhile in her life. Annie was driven by his words and needed to take action but she needed to be patient too. The words of the king were demeaning but it was those words that helped her to unleash her potential, and one day the element of surprise would make him swallow his words. She hoped that he would live long enough to see.

Then one day a mysterious woman from the Eastern Cape paid Granny a visit while Annie and her boyfriend went fishing with his dad. That night Granny told Annie she was going to enrol her in the business college on Monday. Her eyes brightened up with the news but then she asked Granny, where did the money come from?

'All you have to do is to go study . . . don't ask too many questions,' Granny agitatedly said.

'Mama, did you make a loan from the bank?' Annie asked with much concern.

'Loan, my darling? No, child, loans in this country are never granted to non-whites, my friend from the Eastern Cape was here and we made a deal.'

'Did you borrow from her?'

'Go wash. Man, you smell like fish . . . did you catch at least one fish?'

'There are two in the sink. I have already cleaned them, Mama can just fry them.' She made her way to the bathroom to wash up.

The next week, Annie was accepted at the college, and she studied for a junior business diploma. At least with a diploma it will be easier for her to get a job later. Now that she studies, she can only see her boyfriend on weekends because she has a part-time job selling Venda beauty products and he too is still at school. She uses the sample perfumes and make-up so with the result, many people place orders with her because they smell the perfume on her and like it. Every night she goes door to door to introduce the products to people. The commission helps Annie to buy the little essentials she needs. Her uncle and granny are very proud of her and would always boost her confidence.

After obtaining her diploma, she worked in three business companies, where she learned many skills. This is a new era in Annie's life . . . but who is she? Let's step onto the next level and find out as we lift the curtain.

\*\*\*\*\*\*\*\*\*\*\*\*\*\*\*\*\*\*\*\*\*\*\*\*\*\*\*\*\*\*\*\*\*\*

Lifting the curtain:

Here she is—embarking on a new journey, prepared to dismiss the past and ready to be the creator of her destiny. The past cannot be a part of this new era, therefore she needs to remove the invisible mask, lift the curtain, and give the voice a face. The voice cannot be without a face forever and hide behind a curtain when life gives her such an exhilarating feeling of new hope and a road of freedom. The door of opportunity is opening and darkness is slowly turning into light—it is the beginning of a new venture. So together with Annie we lift the curtain to unmask and put a face to the voice as she introduces herself to the world.

I have walked the mile of much abuse, had a loveless childhood but never gave up on life. My situation is but small, a mere fraction of all the problems in this world. Therefore, it does not matter what I went through—there are many people that are worse off. What matters are the choices I made and one of them is never to hate. What also matters is that I rid myself of all the painful memories—the secret silence I have to break in this book. It gives me a sense of joy to know that I am breaking the silence of what I went through as a child.

I love deeply and I forgive easily because my footsteps are ordered by a higher power. Vengeance will never be mine although I did sometimes nurture the wrong seed to taste the sensation of hate. I am not shy to say that at times I liked it and I even had devious thoughts how to kill the man who tried to imprison my mind. With the grace of God, I refrained from doing so because I watered the good seed. It was easy to buy rat poison over the counter—yes, I had the feeling to do that and to poison his tea that I had to make. I did hate him at times and not lightly—I hated him with a passion. Judge me if you like but I am honest in what I say and I write what I know. But agree with me that it has to come out that what you go through in life does not have to stop your dreams from taking flight. Yes, it can put your dreams on hold but it can never decide to change what you want to be in life if you choose to do what is right.

I am just another human who, in my terms, survived the odds. I had a dream and I was inspired by the adverse cursing of a cruel stepfather to dream my dreams. I fed on the painful words and physical abuse to drive me to survive the painful dilemma. I never allowed the cruel, the ugly, and the mean to define who I wanted to be one day. In what was ugly I have seen some beauty too. I cannot hate because within me there is too much love to give. Before I introduce myself to you, may I just add that there is nothing special about me and I am just another ordinary human being who is grateful to my Maker? However, I am not just any face. I am the face who wears the invisible mask. I am like a grain of sand but I believed that it was God who called me by name—I am the voice behind the curtain, Annie Anonyma now the adult. I am that girl with the invisible mask who was hiding behind the curtain and was locked in as a caged bird. Though I missed out on a beautiful childhood, I regret nothing because it was the painful life that has pushed me to be more than just a conqueror. The traumatic life has carved me out of rock and I hope to be the rock that will never break. It is the circumstances of life that moulded and made me strong to survive. To some of you, my situation might be irrelevant, but I know what I had to endure and there is no book that will ever be able to dramatize or describe it. Let those believe who may. I know what I know and even for me it is beyond explanation. I am but a stranger in the land of the living to live out what was already foreordained before the beginning of time. But I am here for a purpose and I have lived long enough to see a victory arranged and prepared by the God who is, was, and is to come, the God I believe in.

Many of my dreams became a reality and most of my goals I have achieved—all this by the grace of God. I do not relive the past though I struggle with it sometimes. The past will always be my stepping stone to live for the sake of completing my journey on this earth. I do not see my stepfather as the king anymore for I believe that he too is here to fulfil a purpose. All I see nowadays is the future and the new choices I will make. My choice now is to forget and to live, stay true to my convictions no matter how high the price. Giving up what I have visualized for my life is not an option because I remain that little girl whose imagination was her powerful force. That little girl believed that one day she would be released from the cage of bondage and walk out victorious. The little girl remains in me.

In 1985 of November, my childhood sweetheart that I vowed to get married to, married me. I thought it was only right to ask my stepdad to walk me down the aisle for my wedding day. His eyes were full of tears, and I knew that it was only respect that can soften the heart of a ruthless man. However, I was not sure if it was the guilt that brought the tears to his eyes, because when I was fifteen years old, he told me that I wouldn't even reach the age of seventeen before I would fall pregnant. He cursed me on that day and I remember how I rebuked his words away from my life. That's when I promised myself to have babies only within a marriage. He was the motivation for me to do what was right, and all his curses and opinions about me became redundant to my hearing. Again I dare to say, his words have carved me out of stone. Some people don't realize that they might push someone, forgetting that the person can push back. I pushed as hard as I could. Anyway, my mother was very proud that I took that stand, and I could see the grateful approval on her face. He proudly walked me down the aisle and gave me over to my husband Joseph.

Nevertheless, Joseph and I did not just fall in love; we vowed to also grow in love. Joseph is a wonderful husband and I love him with my heart. Soon after we got married, we started our own small business. Eight months later, I was pregnant with our first child. I gave birth to a perfect baby girl whom we named Jana. In my childhood I promised myself that one day I would love my children.

Looking at my baby, I cry because of the love I feel for her. Later on as she grows, I will show her the love I have for her. Deep in my heart I still cannot understand why my mother could not love me enough, the way I love my baby, or did she maybe love me in her own way? What made it worse is that my stepfather did not allow my mother to come see the baby or me. All the same, I at least had my in-laws around and my grandmother.

As the years go by, my husband and I are working hard to grow our construction business. At first we were working from home and I did all the office routine while I could keep a close eye on Jana. When I reared Jana from breast milk, I found a reliable person to look after her and the household so that I could help Joseph on sites. We work hand in hand on building sites. He taught me plumbing and tiling; after the tiles are laid, it was my duty to do the grouting. At first it was uncomfortable for me to work with safety gloves. On one occasion, I had enough guts to do it without the gloves. Joseph warned me but I was too stubborn to take his advice. That night I suffered with painful cracks on my hands, a lesson I have learned. I also do glazing and many other small chores like mixing cement or carting the bricks in the wheelbarrow. Joseph teases me by saying I look so cute with my size-4 safety boots and hard hat. On Friday mornings I would do up the wages of the workers, and in those days, it all happened without a computer system. I had to count and place the money in the named envelope of each worker. I had to be accurate with counting. We started off small, but Joseph was a real business guru and could take on anything. I was his partner in life and in business. Later, I went for a few occupational health and safety courses and became the safety officer of the site. We were busy and were blessed with more work. Then I became so busy that I had no time to concentrate on my baby. The one thing in business is, the more work you get, the harder you have to work. We pushed in such a way that we left home early and returned late at night. We had to accelerate because the business was growing and so did the overheads of the company. I was too tired for my baby, and the next morning I was back in the routine. At least I knew that my mother-in-law was also around to help with my baby. This started to concern me and I was unhappy about the situation but the flow of the things could not be disturbed.

But nonetheless, I am in a beautiful place in my life. I have a man who loves me deeply, a man who taught me how to love in return. I am a strong woman who holds many offices. I am a mother, an aunt, a friend, and my husband's wife and business partner. However, it is only human to sometimes get flashbacks about the past. I sometimes talk to Joseph about it and cry. Sometimes we think that we have dealt with the past in silence but bad silence is that which you should break because if you don't it will break you.

With much patience and attention, Joseph would listen and, in his loving way, help me to work through the emotional pain. Nevertheless, all Joseph wanted to see was that his wife was happy, and one day, he decided to slowly teach me to eat watermelon again. I cried and saw that day when my stepfather punished me for 'stealing' meat. Joseph slowly brought a piece to my mouth and told me that if I ate just a piece then I would overcome that which lay buried in my subconscious mind. I refused and the tears rolled down my cheeks but he did not give up. I felt as if I was going back to that day.

'Close your eyes, my baby, and it will be easier because this is a remedy. You can overcome the experience of that day by taking one bite.' I took the bite, cried, and chewed at the same time and I swallowed. I took another bite and another and ate as if Joseph was going to give me marks for it. Then I burst into laughter, and he laughed with me, took me in his arms, and whispered in my ear that it was all over. Watermelon has become my favourite fruit, and Joseph is my darling who helped me to break the power of the bad effects that the watermelon saga had over me.

When I struggle with my past at times Joseph will stretch out his hand to make me stand again.

When Jana was four years old, I became pregnant for the second time and again gave birth to a baby girl, and we named her Yola. Yola was born with complications but those too we overcame, although doctors gave her six months to live. To explain the entire medical intricacies will be a book and a deviation from my topic. With all this said, every hurdle in our lives brought Joseph and me closer to each other. Yola had to undergo a few operations but they were all successful. Together, Joseph and I see our children growing up and our business expanding. As a couple, we are on a path that no one can divert, and Joseph is my most trusted confidant and I owe him a debt of gratitude. We become so busy that I can't even help my children with schoolwork. By the time in the morning when we leave to be on sites they are still asleep; at night when we get home, they are already asleep. Now I really become worried for missing out on their lives because with the load of work, Joseph and I will be on sites even on Saturdays. We made a drastic change and I stayed at home on Saturdays and worked until one o'clock during the week, but then the kids complained that they were missing their daddy. We employed more staff and the load was a bit lighter for Joseph so that he could spend more time with our little girls.

Three years went by and I lost my grandmother. It was my first experience to lose a loved one. I did not handle it well. I felt angry and guilty with myself for not spending enough time with my grandmother. Faced with this sad time in my life, hope had no meaning for me anymore—I felt betrayed by it. In simple terms, hope left me hopeless and angry. I struggled so much with this guilt that two years later, I had to go for counselling to fight off the depression. No one knew that I was in a depression. My husband saw the signs but was in denial. Again, I had to fight to make peace with myself and to forgive myself. The reason why I opt to go for the counselling is that I was too embarrassed to discuss my feelings with family members—I feared their judgments because I was indeed guilty of neglecting my granny. (*For the first time I am saying it and really I am relieved to admit it. That is why I love to write because writing gives one a platform and a voice.*)

My weakness is that I take everything very personally, and some people, even my relatives, know this and will often take advantage of it. However, I cannot help being who I am—it is my persona and to try and change now will be too much of an effort. On the other hand, I am not a walkover either and I can say no when it is applicable. All the same, my grandmother lived long enough to see that I was happily married to the man of my choice and my babies had an opportunity to know their great-grandmother.

# CHAPTER 10

God blessed us in so many ways and I cannot help but admire the way Joseph loves the children and cares about their well-being. He has patience when he reads or plays with them. I see in my husband what I have never seen as a child, in my childhood. Sadly, I have to say it hurts because I never had the love of a father—then again I am happy because my husband is an excellent father to our children and it pleases me. He teaches me not to ponder on what I did not get in my childhood but to give to my children what I never had—and that is love. Every opportunity I get, I hug my babies and kiss them, telling them time and time again how much I love them. I promised myself that I would do that and I am doing it. (They are grown-ups now, but I still do it because they are my babies.)

Joseph is a man who loves peace, with the result he convinces me to visit my mother and my stepdad so that they can build a relationship with our children. I rebel and hate the idea but Joseph always has a way to change my mind. So it became a ritual to visit them every second Saturday. The truth is, it hits me hard inside when I see how my stepdad loves my children. He carries them around, spoils them with luxuries and toys. I observe and I see how he puts them on his lap, wipes the excess chocolate from their mouths, and somehow it breaks the fear in my heart. Is this his way of making up for what he did to me? As for me, I try hard to change towards him. When I am in his company, I feel scared to talk and I am very uncomfortable. Furthermore, he addresses me as his child and that makes me more nervous. He speaks to me with so much respect but all I see are his loveless eyes. Many times I talk to Joseph about the way I feel about my mother's husband but then Joseph rebukes me, but with love. In turn, my babies cry when we have to leave their grandparents, and that makes me feel like the wicked witch in the story. Seeing all this, I think that it is a known fact that change is not only possible; it is also probable. However, I still don't trust it. The fact of the matter is, I always thought that life is like the races I ran in the school sports where the athlete needs to get to the finish line and run through the ribbon, but life does not work that way for me. My line to cross with my stepdad I just cannot finish.

Later, I discovered that my stepdad and mother got baptized and he was ordained as a pastor. They do some missionary work among the underprivileged children and host soup kitchens for them. Tania and Andy are both in high school and help my mother in the afternoons with the soup kitchen. My stepdad is still manipulative towards my mother but she understands him. Their lives have changed for the better but it is hard for me to trust him or my mother. I make all the excuses not to visit them, and Joseph and my daughters would visit them without me.

Needless to say, when I sit in his presence and I hear how he talks about my childhood, it makes me want to scream. In short, one story that really angered me was about the day we went fishing with his friends and their families and how we swam in the Vaal River. The more I listen, the more I feel sick to my stomach because he does not tell the proper story, how he took me in the water, pushed me underneath, and kept his rough hand on my head so that it would be impossible for me to come up for air. Then when he released his hand, I came up, and before I could gasp for enough air, he would push me down again, no time for me to even scream. I felt faintish under the water, and my arms and legs became numb. His friend must have seen what he was doing and came to my rescue. From that day, I had a phobia for water. So this is the scenario and then I am expected to listen to this crap. It is days like these that I sometimes regret feeding and nurturing the good seed that I chose. In truth, oftentimes I think if I had to take revenge to also hurt this man my past was not going to be such an agony to me. But then again, it was not part and parcel of my destiny.

Many times my husband sees my sad facial expression and he knows what it means, then he would simply steer the conversation into another direction, away from the unpleasant subject. Hence, I would look at my mother but she in return looks back at me and has the audacity to smile because she enjoys his stories of lies. To sum it up, the two of them are like little children playing a game, and it is seriously annoying me. Chiefly, this is how I know that there is still no relationship between mother and daughter. Within myself I wonder do I really need this—because in my eyes, my stepdad still gets his way and it is as if everyone is giving him approval. Generally speaking, it is an insult to me sitting and feeling awkward and observing the déjà vu of my childhood. Can I be blamed if I disincline to cooperate? No, my feelings too should be respected. And in any case, why should I subscribe to lies of a reality I have first-hand knowledge of?

On the whole, I sometimes wonder, does my mother ever remember how her husband ill-treated me or has she blocked it out of her memory? It is evident that nothing my stepfather says can give me comfort. To me the damage is done and I work hard through all these emotions. But, having to sit and listen to rubbish and deceitful pretences like this, and be fine with it for the sake of peace and bonding does not gel with me—not now and not ever. It is better for me to not be in their company because now I have to hit the pause button for my mouth not to say the wrong thing, to spare him the humiliation. Why should I contribute to what is said when I live with the truth of what has happened. I said it before: the child never forgets, or should I be deceived by his flattering words because we are all bonding? *Me bonding with him . . . please!* Can somebody please feel me on this one? This is the picture my mother sees as perfect, but for me, I am being hurt all over again. The fact of the matter is, he still runs my mother's life with a heavy hand and she is too blind to see.

Let's face it, my children are bonding with a granddad. I am not sitting in his presence to bond—I am bulldozed to sit here and listen to false statements, lies that take me back to a dark time in my life. So I therefore repeat by saying the stories he tells are what I don't want to hear—period.

Anyway, when we got home one day after visiting my parents, Joseph touched on the topic because I was very quiet. He asked me, did I ever forgive my stepfather? I looked at my husband, said nothing, and walked away. All I can think of are the destructive words of a cruel man's tongue that has almost destroyed my mind. But because of my chosen seed that I nurtured, I am saved. However, deep inside of me I sometimes wonder if I have opened up a wound that was healing. Then Joseph walks after me and repeats the question.

'Did you ever forgive him?' he asked with concern.

'I am not unkind to feel the way I do. When that man talks with so much arrogance and, on top of it, still twists the stories, then it brings something ugly out of me.'

'If you don't forgive him, then the monster will always show its head and reroute you from serving the good seed, my darling,' he kindly said to me.

The rebellion comes up in me and I harshly answer, 'Is it not he who created the monster that now and then shows its head?'

'But it is up to your mind to raise awareness and guard against all hatred.'

'My defence towards him is what he taught me—I am no longer his caged bird and no longer fragile. I am his creation and I bear the fruit of his actions, the child has grown and is strong to fend for herself. He did not break me he made me. The black genuine-leather belt has no rights to my body anymore.'

'You have worked so hard to nurture the good seed and now you divert and take on the persona of the bad seed. This will throw your thoughts in a different direction and it pains me to see you like this.'

'Look, it is pretty basic—I cannot adhere to the twisted stories he is telling my children, it is all lies—he was never a father to me . . . and you know it. I was his slave, I even had to clean the peanuts for him.' I laughed and asked my husband, 'Did I ever tell you that story?'

'It is all in the past now, my baby.' He touches my arm and gently rubs it. It is something he always does to assure me that it is okay.

'This is an imperfect world we are living in, Joseph, and I am not perfect. It is just human for me to sometimes expose my imperfections.'

My husband smiles at me with so much gentleness. 'I know one thing, you are a perfect wife and a loving mother and that means the world to me.'

My husband always has his way with me because he understands me and would always have the appropriate words at the right time to soothe me. So no matter what I feel inside and how all these emotions pain me, at least I have a partner in my life that loves me unconditionally. Therefore, God's plan for my life is what prevails—that is my sealed faith and I shall not be driven by the passion of revenge.

Nevertheless, my husband and I know that in this life we all are given a certain amount of time to prepare for our lives and future. With the result we work hard preparing the way forward. By the grace of God, we do well in our business, grow daily in love and our marriage—as we see our daughters growing up into gentle young ladies.

Joseph and I took a break to the Eastern Cape, and I had to discover something that was kept secret for many years. I rushed back to Johannesburg to confront my mother. I went to see my mother and told her what I saw and what I suspected. According to my knowledge, my father was living in the Eastern Cape—I met him the time I lived there with his family when I had to finish the school year. So I told my mother I met a man that looks exactly like the man whom she says is my father.

'This man you met . . . what did you say was his name?' my mother asked with excited interest and I told her the name. Because my mom and I were alone, she broke down and burst into tears. I sat with my confusion and waited for her to explain me why she was crying.

'My child,' my mother said through her tears, 'for all the years you questioned me, wondering why don't I leave here, and you asked me several times, why did I have to go through such abuse? I always told you it is for you to finish school, yes, that was true but it was not the only reason.' Shocked and with much anticipation, I waited to hear the second reason.

'You see, that man you met is my own child, your brother, and my son.' Wow! This came as a hard punch and I couldn't get a word out. My mother went on to explain and words failed me. Therefore, all I could do was to obediently sit and listen.

'That is the reason why I could never give you to Granny, because that child of mine I had to give away on the seventh day after having him and I promised myself that no one would take you away from me. I know his name and date of birth. The last time you and I ran away to Eastern Cape, I was allowed by his adopted family to see him and I couldn't say anything to him because he did not know. For years I was crying inside because your stepdad does not know about it. If he can find out, he will probably kill me.' I have never seen my mother like this, and I decided to ask the question.

'Would you like to see him now that he is a man?'

'I would give my life just to see that boy again before I die.' Approving of what she said, I nodded. Another piece of the puzzle was fitting in. Above all, it is a question I have had for so many years, thinking how selfish my mother is, and in the meantime she was suffering in silence—alone. It shows one how we as humans can sometimes run with assumptions without knowing the facts. All these years, I watered a seed in my mind that my mother was selfish and thought of herself only. Now the truth came out just to prove to me that my fears had no basis in fact. As a result, I wasted energy, tears, and time. In other words, I was bleeding for all the wrong reasons.

Nevertheless, my mother explained the whole story to me, about being young and how she had to protect our father. In addition, Mom also brought it to my attention how poor they were, and the family was already financially in trouble and about to lose the house because my grandfather lost his job. That I could remember because of the story my granny told me about having nothing when I was entering into this world. At that time, Granny was the only one who was working, and they were five children at home. I did the math on my own and calculated that my father was ten years older than my mother. What a mess, I thought, but like they say, it is what life is all about—skeletons in the closet. In truth, my mother was protecting the man who impregnated her and it was by her own choice. I looked at my mother and had the urge to ask her if there were more secrets I needed to know about. But seeing her so sad and knowing what I know now, I decided to leave it be. Is it not a common fact that we all make mistakes in life?

A month later, my husband and I went back to the Eastern Cape to talk to certain family members and my brother. Both his adoptive parents had passed away, and I thought it would only be fair for him to meet his biological mother in person. I spoke to my aunt then went to my father's widow, and we were given the green light. One of my cousins was good friends with my brother but never knew that their fathers were actually blood brothers. This world is big and round but surely it can sometimes be a small place. My cousin took us to his house, where she was a frequent visitor.

When we arrived at my brother's home, his wife was there but he was not in. We waited and my cousin who normally visited them introduced us and we first had small talk for the sake of conversing. Subsequently, it wasn't long for me to take it upon myself to explain to his wife why we would like to see her husband. Surprisingly she told us that he was battling for years about the same situation—always questioning why he looked so different from his other siblings. We remained for a while waiting for him but unfortunately we had to leave and made the appointment for another day. In the meantime, I was so anxious to meet my own brother, and that night, sleep did not come easily.

Later that week, my cousin arranged another appointment, and we went over to see my brother to clear this matter. To begin with, I have never seen a man crying so much and begging that he would like to meet his mother. Later on, I explained to him about the situation of my stepfather and that I would arrange for us to meet with my mother privately. With great pride, he introduced me to his children.

'My children, this is your own aunt by bloodline.' I was close to tears as his children hugged me with passion. Never, and I mean never, did I ever experience such emotions in my life. My brother hugged me, and for the first time, I felt the sense of belonging. By the time we left,

I couldn't thank my husband enough for making all this possible. All in all, I am by far most richly blessed. Again, it was very hard for me to fall asleep that night. Only this time, I must arrange a meeting secretly for my mother to meet her son, and I tried to put a plan together. Be that as it may, it is a silence my mother broke, and yet the silence must be kept from her husband in order to keep the peace. Or should I say, so that he does not kill her. When will she ever make up her mind to draw the line in the sand and walk out of her prison? Then again, it is not my call—it never was. Besides, she is the one that needs to put her foot down. Currently, I am just the mediator between her and my new brother.

All things considered, I now have to play my role not only as my mother's daughter but also my brother's sister. A month later, my brother was in Johannesburg with his family. My stepdad attended a church conference, and that gave us the opportunity for my mother to meet her son. To begin with, never in my life have I experienced such an emotional anguished moment. Furthermore, I saw mother and son holding each other and crying bitter tears—of joy. Finally, the long-lost son is back in his mother's arms and the mother's dark days now give off a beam of light. The broken piece of her heart has now been restored. The long-awaited years and a dream come true . . . a mother's prayer and here I stand blessed to see what I see.

His wife and children too take their places together, and I see a family cry as if the world is going to end. I see a meeting that was foreordained by the Almighty and now he is observing the moment of joy and I on the other hand observe the essence of bittersweet tears. If only life could have more moments such as these. However, in all moments there is always the element of surprise. My brother's wife tells me in confidence that her husband has a child whom he has denied. I calculate and realize that the child I now know about is my mother's first grandchild and that I am her aunt. I will have to make another trip to go and look for my niece. It will be a different phase of the journey.

After many months of enquiring about my brother's daughter, my Aunty Viola, a God-fearing woman whom we all loved dearly, tells me that this child is in Oudtshoorn in the Western Cape. Aunty Viola is so proud of me and tells me that I am doing the right thing to bring all the broken pieces together for mending. On the other hand, she speaks highly of Blanch (my brother's child), and it gives me some eagerness to meet Blanch. Meanwhile, Aunty Viola prepared Blanch for my visit, and my children want to go with me to meet Blanch and to support me.

Later that same year, we were on our way to go and meet our long-lost relative Blanch. As usual, my husband again made all the arrangements. That is to say, my husband is always ready to support and protect me.

# CHAPTER 11

Meeting Blanch—my mother's first grandchild

It was a long and tiring trip to the Western Cape but we were surrounded with such immaculate beauty as we drove through the Swartberg Pass. Somehow, my mind travelled back way into my past, when the king took us on holiday to Cape Town. We came through this very same mountain pass, and I remember how intrigued I was with these mountains. One way or the other, I fell in love with mountains. Of course, it was a different time then because it was beauty and sadly, because of the king. So then, here I am again to journey through the same route but with a different flavour. It stands as proof that yet again I am obsessed with this stunning beauty of what my eyes behold. The vast high mountains are the real highlight, gracefully standing and showing off their unique loftiness. It is indeed a pleasant show for the human eye. Joseph stopped the car at one of the rest stops for us to climb out and view this immaculate scenery. I watched how my children enveloped themselves with this thrilling experience and the dynamic collage of views. I pause for a moment, stretch out my arms to breathe in the fresh mountain air of this angelic scene of tranquillity. Then I take four steps forward and wonder about the many feet that step on the very ground I am now standing on. As my gaze goes to the direction of the mountains, I wonder how many eyes have looked upon this beauty. What comes to my mind is that man fears time but I should think that time fears these mountains because they proudly stand firm. The truth is, if I had faith enough to command them to move, I am sure they would. Amazed by the beauty of the azure western sky, I am suddenly loaded with a can of new attitude and ready to face my task of meeting my long-lost relative. As I continue to look up to the top of the massive mountains, the trigger of the mind of the child logs in. I stood still and it was as if time too came to a halt. Undoubtedly, my spirit makes contact with these handsome, stylish, masculine mountain peaks. That being so, I look at them with the eyes of Annie Anonyma's vivid imagination. With a holy silence, these grey mountains stare back at me, looking into my soul as they monitor every second of my heartbeat. They hear me breathe as they scrutinize my every move. I hear them whisper, and I am sure that they remember the child who is now an adult. I am compelled to believe in this very moment that life remains a mystery.

I feel humbled and small yet important because my eyes behold the handwork of the Creator. His immensity is beyond what I can explain, and as for this moment in time, it will remain in my heart forever.

We all got back into the car to continue with our journey but the exquisiteness of these mountains did not stop. For the most part, our eyes followed the contours of mountains and valleys through the car windows, and Joseph was kind enough to drive slowly so that our curiosity could be appeased. Subsequently, these tall 2,000-meter-high mountains are so breathtaking that they bring about a warm feeling inside my body that has a calming effect on me. Predominantly, it is only the beauty of nature that can bring such an effect. I was at long last so intrigued by such spectacular beauty, and words cannot adequately describe the phenomenon of this natural elegance. My soul connects with this splendour, and again I feel insignificant in the intensity of this moment. This is my epoch, and it will be added to my history that I might never experience again in the way I do now.

Then, I was taken away from my perfect moment when I heard Joseph's voice saying that we were not far anymore. My focus went back to Blanch, and I wondered, how am I going to break the ice? At the same time, I was on the edge of my seat. On the other hand, what impact will this now have on her life? But deep down, I knew that a piece of her puzzle would also match. I was sure in my heart that she too was looking for answers to fill every void in her life. We heard only good stories about her and that she was a devout Christian, and as an aunt, I can honestly say it pleased me.

Blanch's mother was an employee at the local lodge where we booked ourselves in. Joseph and I had at least some time to talk to her about Blanch because Blanch was still at work and would come later to meet us. She was very transparent and spoke freely.

Apparently my brother called Blanch a few days ago to tell her the date we would arrive; I was very surprised. According to Blanch's mom, her child was very excited but also nervous now that she was going to meet her family for the first time. So somehow she already knew about us, and that would make my job easier. All she really needed now was to meet us in person.

Later that afternoon Blanch came to the lodge. What a beautiful soul, I thought to myself. She was stout and looked a lot like some of the other ladies in the family. Surprisingly, she even walked like them. It is amazing how blood can attract blood, and I couldn't help but see the emotions running through her mind. I introduced her to my kids, who were prepared for this and went out of their way to make her at ease.

'Blanch, these two young ladies are your cousins,' I said as they hugged each other with great acceptance.

'At last the day has arrived for us to meet, and we are very happy to have you back in your rightful place—our lives,' came the words from the mouth of my daughter Jana. This was a profound message to Blanch that we would be part of her life. In any case, we tried to make Blanch feel comfortable by just talking about Oudtshoorn so that we don't come across as overbearing. In return, Blanch was suggesting places we should visit before we go back to Johannesburg.

Her mom was also there and I think that made it more conducive to mental ease. However, somehow she came across as confident with us and I found it to be very brave. Her mother warned us that she would be shy, but I was amazed by the many questions she asked us with ease. Joseph was preparing the fire for a braai while Blanch helped my girls to butter the rolls and spice the meat. In any event, it gave me great joy to see how they were interacting and making small talk. In the meantime Blanch's mom and I talked about my brother.

Later during the meal, when all was calm, I decided to chat a bit to Blanch. When the time was right, I took the lead to break the ice and gently spoke.

'Blanch, my mother is your granny, and you need to know that when you were born, I became an aunt because you are the first grandchild.' Blanch gave me a smile of approval and then my children also started telling her about the saga of how her father met my mother for the first time. Because Blanch was already an adult and could understand things better, we were quite surprised with the way she answered.

'Which means he too went through some major emotions in this life. Sometimes we think life is unfair, not knowing that many people have to deal with situations like these and sometimes even worse.' I was blown away by her wisdom and patience.

'What we fail as humans is to realize that our lives are foreordained by God. I am very glad you came to look me up, and I will appreciate it forever because now I can learn more about my roots.' I saw the gratitude in this God-fearing young woman's eyes, and it made me proud to be her aunt. We spoke long into the night, and by the time Blanch left, I was convinced that we were now a family.

Blanch came to visit us in Johannesburg, and she met her grandmother. My mother grew very fond of her. From then on, she took leave every year to visit us. Blanch and I are very close to each other, therefore we work through many of our pains and fears together and make up for all the lost time. Needless to say, I am not only the proud aunt but I am blessed to have her in my life because she is a child with a gentle spirit and a patient heart. Blanch's presence nourishes me in many ways that I cannot describe. She has pains deep inside but works better with her emotions now that she knows her roots. The evidence of her tears that carve the deep emotional pains that she had endured for years is what brings out the best of who she really is. I am sure, in her heart she knows that divine mercy is what works for her, and this I know by the way she speaks so highly of her father even though he has never been a father to her. That is to say, she reminds me so much of myself, easy to forgive those who had wronged us. All these emotions, I believe, are what build her character and shape her into the phenomenal being whom I cannot help but love with the greatest of merit. Now that she has found the new discoveries of the secrets of long ago, I celebrate with her. I can only wish that she will surrender and find the peace she deserves. As for me, in my eyes she is a magnanimous lady.

# CHAPTER 12

So the years are going by, my daughters are now teenagers and I see how much they love their grandparents—insomuch that I now get schooled by my firstborn. She tells me how unhappy it makes her to see how cold I am towards her grandpa. I was then obligated to tell my children about my childhood, for them to understand my hostility towards my parents. Yola took it very hard, but Jana told me that she really couldn't hate her granddaddy because of his past mistakes. She broke my heart when she said that he was trying hard to make amends by loving them and doing for them what he had never done for me and that was to love them. Hearing them out, I promise that I would work through all my emotions and handle the situation with a difference. Jana also tells me I preach to them about the good seed, yet I cannot forgive. Those words made an impact and I asked myself, who am I to judge? For this reason, I take time to think and remember how I say I have enough love to give, yet I cannot find it in my heart to love the man who has raised me. Now I know that I am contradicting myself over and over again.

Then, in July 2007, my stepdad became very ill and was diagnosed with cancer. His sickness really was an opportunity for me to change my ways towards him. I saw a sick man and I played my role, as a daughter should. By then, Jana obtained her driver's license and would visit him every second day. Once a month she would go with him to the hospital for his monthly check-up. Basically, in myself I see my humanity—I don't see what he did to me in the past anymore. The truth is, all I see is a very sick man who is the only father I have ever known. I see the man who has clothed and fed me, paid for my education, and provided a roof. My heart breaks to see him go through so much pain—no human deserves such pain. Moreover, as the months go by, we all support my tired mother because my stepfather's health is deteriorating. When I saw how Jana cares for him, it made me realize that my child really loves him. She feeds him with patience, washes him, and dresses him. Even his hair she would wash and brush. All this brings out the soft side in me, and I realized this is really who I am. I am soft-hearted, never aggressive and I have a forgiving spirit because I love the human race.

One day my mother called me to tell me he was very weak and was struggling to eat. I went there, took some yogurt, and fed him. When I was finished, he asked me not to leave the room. That was the day he asked me to forgive him for all the wrong he had ever done to me. With a weak, trembling hand, he took both my hands, and with tears in his eyes, he told me that he had also asked God to forgive him. Tears rolled down his skinny cheeks, and I got up from my chair, took his frail, skinny upper body in my arms and kissed him on the top of his head. At that moment again it was a proven fact that change is not only possible but also probable. The change was the forgiving spirit within me. I did not hate him, but up until that day, I never forgave him. Then on that day, the world stood still for a moment just for me, still standing in silence, holding him, forgiving him, and thanking God for the moment in time. I thanked God for my existence in this universe, and I embraced my purpose in life—there is a fundamental purpose when we forgive. As usual, forgiveness is life and the beginning of wisdom—the first step to conquer bitterness. Assuredly, bitterness rots the hearts of humans, and it is the root of an evil that will refuse to let the heart forgive.

On the fifteenth of December of that year, Joseph and I had to go to Durban. I phoned every now and then to hear about his well-being. My mother informed me that some days he was okay and other days he was weak. In the meantime, all we did was pray for him. On the twentieth of December, my mother phoned me to notify me. She pleaded with me to return to Johannesburg because my stepdad had taken a bad turn. We prepared to leave Durban early the next morning, but later that day, he died on his way to the hospital. We rushed back to Johannesburg to assist my mother.

We assisted my mother to prepare for the funeral and notify all his family. It was at a very difficult time because it was the weekend of Christmas. Therefore, we could only have the funeral on the twenty-seventh. It was very emotional for my daughter Jana when everybody had the chance to say his or her last goodbyes at the coffin. By the time I stood at the coffin, I looked and no tears could roll from my eyes—all I saw was the face of the man who raised me, because he was not my foe and in my heart I had peace. To me it was an attractive way to say goodbye—the end of the pace.

After the funeral, we cleaned up and locked my mother's house and took her home with us. Joseph and I then decided after Christmas that my mother should hire out her house and live with us. My mom was very happy about the decision and thanked Joseph.

Nevertheless, my life has changed tremendously, and for the first time, I feel I have a mother. Evidently, this new future works well with me because now I build and strive to a new and better history for my life. The children too adapt to having my mother around who now can be nothing else but herself. My mother and I are bonding well, and I see a motherly persona that I could never see in her before, with the result she takes over the kitchen and household and I enjoy seeing her so free and happy. Her cooking and order around the house is highly appreciated. I go on my travels with Joseph, and she takes care of everything while we are away from home. I become so close with my mother, and every now and then, I tell my kids how I fear if something should happen to her. My daughters reassure me that God is never unfair and that I should rather concentrate on the time we have to love one another again. I do so and thank God every day for the opportunity and grace to still have my mom, whom I so often despised when I lacked understanding. I am healing from my past, but at times, I still ponder and think back; I guess it is only human because our history is there to follow us. Whichever way, now that I have my mother who is a real mother to me, I can only regard myself as fortunate. How the wheel of life has changed and somehow I feel free from the pains of my past, or so I thought. On the other hand, my mother is free to say whatever she needs to say without having to count her words or fear a backhand from someone who does not approve. Together we go on holidays, and so we make up for all the tears and wasteful years we lost. It sure is true when people say that this life wants to be lived.

# CHAPTER 13

With the passage of time, all things in our lives are bright and beautiful until one day when my mother dropped a bomb that changed my life unexpectedly. Vulnerable and confused, I get access to yet another skeleton that was hidden in the closet of almost-forgotten time. Is there ever going to be an end to all the hidden secrets? Will I forever have to stand guard and be ready to either fight or stand aside to make way for the big reveal? Is there no mercy in this life for me? Will this be the last of the trump cards that come with the unexpected unpleasant detail, or should I say the last nail in the coffin? Where will it end and does it have an end? Has gravity bypassed me, or am I just another oddball who needs to understand the underlined? Is this the unexpected meteor that's now going to strike me? Is it the final bomb, no, the atom bomb—going to be released? Okay, no more suspense, here it is.

My mother tells me that my brother's father is not my father. What do you the reader say—Ja, right, what is the big deal? The big deal is she deceived me for many years to believe a lie. The big deal is that this is a joke, and yet I am not laughing because I am here but I don't feel as if I exist.

When she strikes with this bomb, I jump up from the chair I was sitting on and I take on my African roots.

'Eish! Joh . . . why—hiboh!' Yes, I can say all these words because I am an African woman. Born on the African continent—yes, I am proudly South African, and when we go into shock, then these are the words we use. I am in dire shock right now and very confused. I return to the chair, sit down, and look my mother straight in the eye—and I ask, 'Then who is my father?'

As usual, in life we all want to trust but sometimes we never know because trusting too much can come at an unexpected price. How long do I have to adapt and cope with disappointment? How many times do I have to embrace the changes and guard against war with myself? Will there ever be a time for me not to just live above the line of my own thinking and just live? Right now I am the captain of my ship but I am steering it trough rough waters. The waves are big and the storm is fierce, but I am going to steer this ship with my skills for the sake of my crew and my sanity.

My mother sat with us to talk and to break down the final walls of her pain and secrets. But, this crackdown is the start of new pain for me. What she is now offloading is what I upload. I looked at the faces of my daughters and my husband (my crew)—trying hard to be the three pillars of support. On balance, I somehow feel proud of them because their patience, love, and understanding they display are because they do it for me. My daughters are slowly becoming like their mother—they too are feeding the good seed. They sit and listen with readiness and are not merely discouraged by what they hear. In essence, my family now are standing in the gap, ready to protect what is rightfully theirs—their mother.

I grinned because my ears and mind are taking an assault with what I hear from my mother. In short, what I hear is traumatic and it somehow alters my persona. I am agitated and also embarrassed. Apparently, the mysterious lady who paid for my business diploma was my grandmother—my *real* father's mother. When I was in high school, she came to Johannesburg to take me to the Eastern Cape but my mother refused because she was not prepared to lose another child. All these thoughts running through my mind are so tiring and I feel disappointed that my granny kept this from me. My mother explained that they were protecting me. Protecting me! I closed my eyes thinking, 'Protecting me—has my mother no shame? I had to go through such a bad childhood because she gave her firstborn up and was scared to lose me. However, it was guilt that led her to the selfish motives and piled-up secrets, and yet I had to suffer. Hence, it was her husband that caused my *childhood suffering*. I was the human sacrifice. I was punished for the dark secrets of my mother's life and she had the audacity to call it *protection*. I felt like getting up and walking away from this intimate family meeting. But I cannot do this now because my crew will suffer the assault. For a few months, I ate honey and now I am back to golden syrup again, and my history takes on another page of an adverse report.

What I hear from my mother is such a hard punch for me and I feel too weak to deal with it. My skin is being removed from my face. However, I like the fact that my mother is coming clean to reveal the truth. Maybe my stepdad was right when he said that I have no sense of belonging. I am not sure who I am and where I come from. Let me rephrase it. Do I know who I am? Yes and no. Why, because my mind is still cluttered with a mixture of suspicions about the truth. Is it the right time to spark off a debate? No, now is not the time, for the sake of my own stability. However, I am not anymore in the desperation of wanting to find the answers that would yield to my questions. The fact of the matter is that the truth will always have three sides. I therefore make peace with the knowledge that maybe one day only time will serve to reveal the revelation. It is indeed now matter-of-factly that I think of no reason why I should not get on with my life.

Notwithstanding, all these years I fought hard not to turn myself into damaged goods, slowly dying inside, longing to be free. In whatever way, now that I am supposed to be happy and stable, I become frail and fractured in my soul. Deep inside of me, I yearn for solitude because before I yearned for answers only. However, now that I know the answers, I am more confused. Now I have to steer my ship through the high tide of troubled waters. I want to see all well and happy and everything in place. I am the peacemaker because peace for everyone depends on me. I offer a sacrifice but I am that sacrifice. I try to still the pains of others but I pain inside. I treat the wounds of many but my own I cannot heal. I dry the tears from many cheeks yet no one sees mine. I uplift, lead, and guide yet I am lost. Though I am surrounded by many who love and care for me, I am still alone with the wounds of my soul in my own quiet corner, in turn, fighting the battles of my mind—lost and alone. In short, this is my standing on the battleground bleeding to survive the troubles of my mind.

So as I am writing this now, I am also crying because I am going deeper into my soul. After all, it is a place where I figure that I have imploded my feelings and somehow this is how I am exploding. In other words, all these years I was under the impression that I have dealt with these feelings but I only realize now that I have bottled it up in a deep and dark place. Not knowing that that dark place was my place of secrecy while I became a fugitive of the walls of my mind.

This is a side of myself I have never met before but now I know that it is my essence and a part of my identity. What does it say to me? It says that I am a sensitive woman who needs to cry and free my mind with the help of my tears. Nonetheless, these tears are painful and it leaves a throbbing bulge in my throat. I cry these tears and it reminds me that my life is a reality. Be that as it may, I am not sure if I am half human because it seems like the human race is hard to trust. My tears want to make me even lose trust in my ability to stand firm. Now I question all my hard work for working together with my mind never to lose hope. Then people say I am crazy when I whisper my deepest feelings to the sun or call the wind my friend. They stare at me when I hug a tree to feel its warmth. In the eyes of humans, I need therapy but for me to connect with nature is my therapy. Nature does not surmise my thinking—it works with me.

The best time for me to think is now and it is three in the morning and I connect with myself while everyone in the house is asleep. I cry by myself, because the one thing I hate is for people to see me break. Tears, to many, can be seen as a sign of weakness and not as a time to offload the baggage. Tears bring healing to the mind, heart, and soul. However, I question myself and wonder, did I perhaps put the invisible mask back on my face because deep inside I am really yelping and silently suffering? The truth is, I feel beaten and bruised by the billows of life. This is the deep crying out but I know there is a deep to hear and see. Indeed, there is a time for everything, and now it is my time to cry and feel this deplorable grief. I am one with it and have to work through it. I cry but somehow I am not even sure why I shed these bitter tears for the absence of the presence of my earthly father. That is to say, I never had one and I have never experienced such love. What benefit is there in all this weeping now when I grew up without the love of a daddy? What ignorance is this to succumb under this dreadful situation? What happened to the strong woman I used to be—where did she go? She is still here but she is bleeding because she is a human with a soul. So through all the shadows of my past, today is the day that I shall realize that there is a part of me that I am introduced to and I shall accept it. In conclusion, tomorrow will be a day of new beginnings, and I will transcend the future and my thoughts with new hope and a different mind shift. The challenge is to face the new changes, adjust with them, and overcome. It is a smart way to contribute to the battles of my own mind, but I am aware that it will not be easy. Nevertheless, my crew will be the perfect support system to help me work through it all. My family is my only real wealth; they always restore my life to its former blessings. Dark clouds will remove themselves because they cannot stay in the same position forever. They will move in order for me to see the sun—the same with life, every day there is a new phase. The fact of the matter is, sometimes one has to walk away from that which you cannot solve or change. Chances are that it might pain you, but maybe that is the pain that you need to actually heal from. Refusing to let go will only make you dread over what you cannot blame yourself for. I hope and pray that I can heal.

The next day, Joseph and I had to go on a trip to Namibia. I was very eager for the trip because it was what I needed. We had all our bags ready and were about to go. Unfortunately my mother collapsed and struggled to breathe. We rushed her to hospital and were told that she had an anxiety attack. I realized that it was difficult for her to come clean, and it had a bad effect on her health. Of course, I felt bad for thinking that I was the only one suffering, how selfish of me. My mother remained in hospital for four days, and we later learnt that she actually had a slight heart attack. All these years of bottling up—a secret silence she could not break because of the circumstances. Now that the silence has exploded, it still comes with its damages. We have almost lost my mother and truly it was eye-opening for me that life is too short not to appreciate her.

Later that year, the whole family went together to Namibia and my mother enjoyed the trip. We had enough time to talk, and I was patient to lend a careful ear and not judge my mother for her past. No doubt, I realized that I am blessed to at least learn the truth and give my mother a chance to voice her ordeal. So now that I know it all, I know that we need to do some serious recycling and remove all the trash. I do not exclude from my mind that all trash is not necessarily bad, and it can be another blessing in disguise, with the result I had enough time to think of my next step and decided to look up the whereabouts of the mysterious man my mother said is my dad.

When we returned to South Africa, I threw myself into my work, trying hard to forget about the dad I have never met. I travel with Joseph regarding new projects in Lesotho to sidestep the hunting for my dad. The truth is, I was scared about any new findings. Anyway, no one knows I am dodging in fear of disappointments. I am busy with my husband, attending many meetings to negotiate business matters, with the result I am still trying not to think of the new changes in my life. Meanwhile, I struggle to work through these new feelings. At least, the other father I have met and had an inkling where I stood. But these new changes threw me completely off balance, and it is so embarrassing. I am under the constant surveillance of my family. They see the inflicted emotional pain I try so hard to endure and hide, but they are too scared to touch the topic in fear that it might anger me. In truth, I know this is a situation that I must confront and simply get done with it, but the fear of rejection is ever so present. Who says the so-called father wants his life to be changed now, and I don't want to be the one to go and disrupt any family with my baggage. As it is, in my eyes it is not fair and there is no willingness within me to do so. All these mind battles are not easy to deal with; although I pretend to be fine, I know it is holding me captive.

# Chapter 14

So after forty-seven years, I am being presented with the truth—the amazing truth—and this truth sucks. For this reason, I realize that I have only one option in all of this, with scrambled thoughts and a disorientated mind of the sudden turn of my life. The option is to accept the change of the situation. The fact of the matter is that I am nothing but an illegitimate love child of my parents. Needless to say, I cannot help but think that I am a product of an arrangement. I am bold enough to laugh because it is what it is. Nevertheless, I am left with nothing but a description of my 'father' in his younger days and a few photos. I also learnt that I have a sister in Eastern Cape and a brother who passed away. Will I go on to yet another phase of my journey and go and look for my father and my siblings? In contrast, this seems to be the new trend in my life nowadays, always having to go look for the long-lost and not realizing how lost I am all my life. No, I won't do that because it is not my plan to shatter people's lives. It will not be fair in any case. Be that as it may, it is enough that I know what I know and I am fine with it. Hence, how sure am I that I am fine with what I know? Let's face it, maybe I only convince myself that I am fine and have accepted the idea—until it will surface again.

Nonetheless, all my life I tried to find myself while so many pieces of the puzzle were kept away from me. Why is it that I don't feel free, or am I still waiting for my jubilee? Whereas for now, I am the slave of my own thoughts and I am behind the bars of my troubled mind? I am imprisoned by all my emotional pain, and it is the only option I think I have. Overall, if I dare to voice my opinions, I will be accused of hurting many but no one cares how hurt I am. Thus, it is expected of me to keep the peace. I have no right to break or even feel fragile because I am the peacemaker and the victory of everyone. So what is the use if I am to break the silence and still conceal it for the sake of peace? What peace and whose peace? Peace I cannot even lay claim to.

Anyway, for months I am tossing and turning at night. My family notices my silence and seldom sees my smile. Inside, I wrestle with myself and try to replace the shame of not really knowing who I am—with silence. There is this saying they say, silence is golden—but in this silence there is no trace of gold. We need to make peace with the fact that there will always be unfair situations as long as the world exists.

Months later:

While this is the case, after many phone calls and investigation I found out that my so-called father was married and lived in America for a number of years. To my disappointment, he sadly has died. New feelings come to light, and I now really feel robbed because I never had the opportunity to meet or even see the man whom my mother claimed had fathered me. In contrast to my findings, I am having a hard time with this, but I do meet his sister and we grow in a relationship. The cycle has changed, just like my sensei said it would—the wheels of life. As an example, Blanch found her aunt and I have found mine. Furthermore, I have learnt to love this aunt of mine because she is the only connection I have with my father and she means everything to me. Whether this picture is true or false, I don't know and I don't care. If it is false, then I will live in this fantasy, be that as it may. Whatever, my life was in any case one big lie. So what am I doing now? I go with the flow. However, somehow I still feel the void and I try hard to ignore what I sense. Anyway, this aunt—well, we see each other at least once a month, and when I see her, the waves of belonging overflow in me. If in fact it is the truth I am feeling, then again I find the beauty in the ugly; no more yearning because I do belong somewhere. This is indeed if I am honest with myself. Do I really say it with pride because my aunt always tells me that we have each other? She has accepted it and I still question it. In essence, right now it feels so right yet I still feel that there is still something amiss about the calculations of the time. Anyway, for me these words she humbly says to me with so much compassion. And, for me these are golden nuggets on a platinum tray. Moreover, she also tells me many things about my father, and again I hear that I have a sister in the USA. Will that be another journey for me to go on to and look for her? I don't know and I don't think so; I am too tired for all of this searching business.

If I have to say something, then it will be. The known fact in life is that we are here to fight for everything and sometimes everyone. Everything that we think we own, someone's trust, patience, understanding, tolerance, acceptance, assurance, appreciation, and sometimes love—only to find that these are merely components of what life holds, and yet we think it's a special rank of some sort of understanding. We want to see life the way we think it should be. Commonly, we don't guard against disappointments and hidden agendas that can unfold in a twinkling of an eye. To illustrate, we live to build and take time to do it, but it can take only one unfavourable incident to break it down within minutes. A bomb is thrown at you, so the damage is done and there goes your building up in flames.

Therefore, in this life there is no way we can build up any survival skills to be prepared for emotional pain. It is careless to say we are prepared for the unexpected. Let's face it—we are never prepared. When whatever strikes, when it strikes—then it has arrived unannounced. It comes in many different ways and forms. It might come via sickness, pain (both physical and emotional), poor health, defeat, trauma or disappointments, death of a loved one, and these are but a few. Furthermore, each of what I mention still has long categories under their own lists. Thus it is, the worst thing that I always have to fight is my painful ugly past but one day I am going to stand up against it. Stand up to fight back. The challenge now is to deal with it and how to do so. The question is, will I ever find closure? I can only say it is another matter entirely that needs to be seen.

To point out, I once heard that the greatest fear of mankind is the fear of pain and death. However, I think mankind has outgrown these fears and can sometimes become immune and lose the war and allow either their minds or bodies to shut down. They no longer fear their own oblivion. Based on our circumstances, life is a continuance of many fights. We fight for our rights, fairness, and our honour. We fight for a recovery from many different issues. But then again, it is only what I think and say.

We fight to strive and strive to succeed. We fight for acceptance and pardon, yet it's hard for us to easily forgive at times. Pointed out, we say we forgive and forget, yet we have lapses of memory when we remind others of their previous mistakes. We point fingers at others, forgetting that three of our own are pointing back at us. We fight to please others and are pleased with the acceptance and think it is honoured. Perhaps we are actually fighting to exist. So they say this is life, but I say this is but a page in the manual of the workbook of life. Or, are we merely determined souls always battling with our own circumstances? Who knows?

In all due fairness, we talk, complain, and think too much. Maybe, just maybe, we need to become quiet and observe a little longer before we continue to analyze all the constituent parts of what we see, think, hear, and complain about. That is why I don't like the title of CEO (chief executive officer)—because of the entitlement you have that other so easily question without thinking. As observed, people question your ability as a leader, forgetting you are following the protocol of the workbook of the company. Some refuse to be managed, and really the fact of the matter is that we will never be able to manage people. It is indeed evident; all humans have their own ideas and come from their own backgrounds which we know nothing of, and their stubbornness is because of what they had to endure in the past. We can't blame them; they have their own survival skills and defence strategies. The fact of the matter is, not all out there feeds the good seed. Now if you try to lead or discipline them, they regard you as a little Hitler of a new era. I speak out of experience because I used to be like that, not open to good advice from anyone. Not ready to learn from others. I used to like saying 'Do these people know where I am coming from? They don't know me.' Yes, we are all up against the world.

Later in my life, I have learnt to love the word CEO, because I became the CEO of my own life. I lead, apply, remove, and discipline myself as I am slowly running the race with the horses. Not winning yet—I am but a novice on the tracts of the experienced but I will get there. Humans have a tendency to always bring up their toxic past, but we convince ourselves that we don't want to live in it. Nevertheless, we authorize the past to follow us like a shadow and to be the crutch we want to lean on. Sorry if this does not apply to you; not all in this world are misfits—I am. And, I know the words I write are going to land in the hands of the critics, but then again who doesn't criticize? It is not a human error; it is a human habit. All my life I have been criticized, so what difference will it make now? I have a saying: "*If the adverse words of a few did not kill me, then I am alive.*" All others are irrelevant.

Here I am; I fought many years for a sense of belonging and acceptance, crying privately alone on the inside. Trying hard not to show it on the outside, but the invisible mask hides it. Smile on the outside and frown on the inside. I am unique in my own special way because I live but sometimes I die a thousand times just to live again. Despite anything to the contrary, it is part of what the invisible mask hides. Who can see and who dares to disagree? It is by my choice that on my face, it is I who wears the mask. And as long as I protect that mask, I will suffer in silence. Do I choose this time to ventilate, escape, break, bleed, and delete? Am I lifting the veil for myself to stop trying so hard to be Madam Fix It? In fact, the more I fix, the more I damage myself. I work overtime to do well unto others, and yet some question my good deeds and see what they prefer to see. So I need to remove this mask and show my fears, my pain, my disagreements, and the trials I face on my own. The bottom line is, I am tired of self-talk. That is to say, I want to scream, explode, and be heard. I want to stop ignoring the negative and see some positive in every negative. Hence, I want to be irresponsible so that all can see how responsible I really am. That is to say, I want space to breathe—it's time and I demand it because I deserve it.

For once I want to be human and be allowed to criticize, complain, and make major mistakes for a change. Thus, I want to feel what it's like to be human without having to be perfect. Of course, I want to feel what it's like to live and let live. Yet, the core point is that it is only I who can break the silence, remove the mask, and rid myself of this penalty. Only I can be the judge to free myself from this injustice called second and put myself first for a change. Yes, it is my low ego and I too am offended by it, but for now, it feels good because I am letting steam off. No validation for myself. My world of many dreams is tumbling down just like Humpty Dumpty fell off the wall and had a great fall. I am falling but not further than the ground. The truth is, I am having a dialog with myself and, at the same time, taking my mind on a tour just to feel how it feels to gel with my low self-esteem. To point out, all my life I worked hard through a restrained childhood to see all the fine optimisms and now I fall. To whatever extent, I like this fall because no one can see how I am falling. Meanwhile, no one can read my mind; only God sees my heart. Yes, I expect too much from others, knowing I would never get what I really want. I know that I am the only supervisor to supervise my feelings and my life. In fact, I have programmed it that way, to never expect what I cannot get. It is right; I grew up that way—always obliged for what I dislike but have to accept because of the circumstances, with the result I was never brave enough or even had the right to complain or voice my opinion. My feelings were never taken into consideration; after all, who am I anyway but the face with the invisible mask, not forgetting the illegitimate child who does not know her father. So what I say now is that I want to illuminate the old and have a fresh, clean hard drive and start over. Vacuum the floor of my mind and come to the realization that my soul went through a starvation process. Therefrom, I will feed it with the best nutrition, to be equipped with the best survival skills. No more heart palpitations, cold sweats, and bleeding sores. The challenge is, is it possible? Well, I am bold to say yes because I am going to love myself hard enough from now on. It is my time, the place, and it is now. Will it be the apex of my new way of thinking, or am I dealing with my prostrations? Is it the right motion followed by the proper intentions to discover another side of who I am—the sorry side, a short decoy, but it exists. It is a matter of my life that I am observing. I am observing my condition, the futility that is holding me back. This is the time I want to rearrange what went wrong, and it is indeed an important process that I need to season with love. To break it down, it is a way to rid myself of this anger and shame I never knew I had.

In contrast, in my opinion, life is like this: it is like a river, sometimes full and the current of the stream is normal. Then at other times, it is dried out by the adversity of bad weather, or should I say an act of God? However, the beautiful water will return to polish the rocks and the slopes, to continue with the journey. Our lives on earth are many journeys we travel, and we are pilgrims passing through in search for the ideal dream to live out our lives. Then again it is only the way I see it and someone else might disagree.

# CHAPTER 15

I have travelled many times too far back into my toxic past. The truth is, sometimes it was only to get a glimpse to review. Maybe, I tried to find some belonging or a shelter but could not find it. Needless to say, the future is where I should look for that hope. In whatever way, I pain myself with what used to pain me, and I get obsessed with thinking how I was hurt, degraded, deceived, mentally abused, and undermined. Primarily, my mental mind is overloaded with flashbacks of my reality, and I am the victim of my own thoughts. I am not realizing that I can never reverse my past to change it. Instead, I keep on rewinding it to review what I know will make me sad. Is it only human for me to wake sleeping dogs and not leave them to rest? Is it fact or is it habit or am I trying to blend with all the broken pieces? Who can tell but time, because in due time I will be healed. At least that is what I believe.

To put it together, if we do not appreciate the company of people who make us unhappy and uncomfortable, then the right thing is to avoid such persons who are a disturbance for the mind. The same should be applied to the past we clearly don't want to remember. The point is, maybe we don't have to go there.

Needless to say, my toxic past is like a hungry predator always ready to reappear, to stalk and devour me. I try so hard to run from it but always end up wounded. Nonetheless, I should learn to stand up and kill this predator before it kills me. I have heard so many times people say, 'Know your enemy and fight back.' Sadly, in my case I do know my enemy but I don't fight back. I allow it to bully me, knowing about the dangerous toxins it holds. This opponent is strong and knows how to break the human spirit within me. All I do is take the punishment and accept defeat. I cannot go on and be unequally yoked with a toxic past that does not bring any value to my life. This pain that hurts me so much should be the pain to change my way of thinking. In essence, in the true sense of the word, I have grown tired of being victimized by my own past and I am ready to take my stand because I deserve to be free. So I have come to the conclusion to have that dialog with my past that I should have had long ago. The truth is, mistakes are there to be rectified and I have made a big mistake to linger on my bad past. Now my mind is made up and I will do what is right. The right thing to do now is to have a dialog with my past.

Dialog with my toxic past:

> Me: I know you for most of my life, you are my bitter past. You rock up time and time again to invade my happiness and leave me with grief. I live but I die a thousand times because you simply reappear. You make me cry and let me go through sleepless nights with many battles on my mind. I am an inmate of my own mind and you are my accuser.
>
> My Past: The truth is, I am the reality of your life and I am here to always remind you where you come from. I never asked for this to happen—it happened and you need to deal with the fact that I am here. The fact, as it may be, is I am your reality and not your accuser. You are the one who always blames yourself for what you have left undone. I am only the bystander, and may I say it again—your reality.
>
> Me: And you are a reality I do not want to remember anymore because this reality comes from the abyss. I was born for a purpose and I have the right to be on this earth to live my life that was granted by a higher authority. Therefore, I have news for you. You have challenged me for the last time because today I am not shattered. Today I am inspired and ready to do what I should have done years ago. You are my bitter past that has intimidated me for many years. My

fear for you has grown in such a way that I could never face you. However, now I have decided not to yield and allow you to imprison my mind any longer. You were my teacher and you taught me well that from every bad, good can come along, and in every ugliness, there is some beauty too. I have found the good in the bad and the beauty in the ugly.

My Past: So why moan if my teachings taught you well? The flashbacks of your life, I bring to you like a wave for you to know that you cannot change the reality of your own life. If truth be told, it was destined to be that way and we cannot fight fate. So do not allow your anger to demotivate you now. You jump from one emotion to the next and forget where you come from. I am the essence of your life, that which you cannot change or rearrange. Take what I do as a good lesson and learn from it. We are partners, you cannot go on without me and I cannot go on without your approval. So just embrace me again and accept that I am here to stay.

Me: Yes, your teachings made me strong enough for me to choose my future pathway and I chose it. My new future starts now and you are not a part of it. The day for you to die has arrived and it is now. I am going to kill you—because I can. And when you are dead, then I will not only be rid of you, I will be free. Insomuch, free to bury you but we will have no memorial service or a special goodbye. I have learnt from you and you made me but I will no longer allow you to break me. You were my teacher but never my leader, my reality but never my choice.

I am the original of who I am and I lay down the law—my law, because if I don't, then I will become a tyrant. So by my own will, I lay down the law of myself for myself and that is that I will no longer be your slave but the master of who I am. Therefore today I face you and with the power of my tongue and the strength of my mind I eliminate you from my life—so die now.

I feel how my past is getting weak and then I see how it surrenders then dissolves and finally dies without fighting back. My command is honoured—it is an instruction, my instruction and the toxic past gave in to the command of my mind. I take my rightful place as the ruler of my own mind, and it is a divine intervention because I have carried out my main objective.

Me: You are dead to me and my future takes on life. Very composed—I am not only taking my life back but also the entitlement of my soul. As I now remove the septic thorn from my flesh and the invisible mask from my face, I declare victory and I am free to return to my purpose and enjoy the hope, achievements, and the many blessings given to me by God. No longer will my mind be abused with the poisonous substance of my past.

Conventionally, this is the date and the time where my fears overcome adversity. And, the emotional suffering is reaching a dead end. I step into this dimension to meet the world for the first time—the rebirth. I embrace the beauty of life with holiness and faith. At the same time, I display the passion of my soul for this victory, as the law of attraction responds to my feelings. However, I am aware that life will not be without problems; I have confidence in the future. As a matter of fact, uncertainty and stress will always be part of life, but life is for the living. The truth is, I will try hard to do what is right and leave my future in God's capable hands.

So now that I have broken ties with my past and remove this invisible mask for good, there is nothing to hide anymore. I am breaking the shackles that bound me for years. My toxic past is dead and buried, gone and forgotten now. In fact, I feel the change in my body and I feel how the pains are getting lighter. There will be no more agony of despair and senseless feelings of guilt. It is a new day with a new time phase for me to open the door for my deserved happiness. No more shadows of a ruptured past because I look at the world with different eyes. The book of the past is closed now. I see a new vision as I am turning away from the old. In my hands I carry the majesty that is in me because the hostage has been released. I now enter through the door of a new future that I know I deserve. This is the future that waited long for me to make the first move.

I cannot control the circumstances of what happened but I can be grateful for many things in my life, things that will change from this day on, and I will value what is good for me. I walk tall and I stand firm on a solid foundation.

Every day I step into my distinction of who I am. And, I willingly accept the fact that I am a phenomenal woman with a purpose in life.

Out of all the vile there are the good I can call up. To begin with, I met my brother and his family, not forgetting Blanch, a long-lost member of our family. I have a husband who loves and supports me. Together we empower many people in our business and in our walks of life. My children adore me, and I have my mother who cares about me now. Tania is still in my life and sometimes serves as an outlet pipe for me. To think that I changed her nappies when she was a baby then she changed the nappies of my babies and now my babies are changing the nappies of her baby. And so the cycle has changed because now I have the opportunity to be a crutch for Tania and I am happy to be a second grandmother to her children. Besides, I enjoy many conversations with my biological father's sister (my aunt) and I have refrained from feeling guilty about my grandmother. Instead, I hold dear what she taught me in life. As for the people who have been my family, they remain my family. That will never change, and yes, little Annie's big dream came to light—she is writing again.

So there is no time to collapse and feel that life is against me. After all, I am working with life and life works with me. I enjoy having my mother around, and my life feels complete with my granddaughter Everlitte. So life treats me well and for now I will live and enjoy who

I am—the strong woman, the wife, mother, grandmother, sister, daughter, aunt and trusted friend. Most of my family is not related to me by bloodline but they are the people I chose to be my family. Yes! I regard myself privileged because I am in my roles with many offices and I have the right to be here. My life is now filled with positive contributions that I embrace with great appreciation. I have forgiven myself for my past and I am now rewarded with good health, harmony, and peace of mind. Daily I teach my emotions to react on positive thoughts only and slowly I am becoming the happy person I always wanted to be.

On 25 September 2012, I celebrated my fiftieth birthday. My husband gave me a big party and surprised me on that night when he gave me the Star of David in the presence of family and friends. I proudly wear that gold chain around my neck. The highlight of that night is when Joseph explained in his speech the meaning of my name and why I was given that name. It was the desire of the Jewish lady who provided all my baby clothes, because my name has a beautiful meaning, and I should be presented with the Star of David as a token of my jubilee on my fiftieth birthday. I am enjoying my jubilee for it was promised to me.

As for my mother, she has become my pillar of strength and I enjoy every moment and every heart-to-heart talk I have with her. The many battles of my toxic past I have dismissed, and I refuse to relive them again. Like I said earlier on, that book is closed. I feed on the many positive contributions and I learn to handle difficult situations with positive wisdom. My quest for happiness in this life I pursue with diligence. My vision is renewed and my passion for life is fresh. I have wings to fly and nothing is going to take me back to the yesterdays of my life.

However, I practice empathy so that I don't step on the boundaries of my mother's feelings. No matter what happened, she is still my mother and I would never disrespect her for her past or, for that matter, let others do so. I remind myself that it was in her womb I was housed for nine months and I fed from her breast milk. For now, I enjoy solitude and I am grateful for the truth that made a difference in my life. I know what I know now but I am not going to stay stuck in it. I am moving on—we all bleed to survive in this life and then we survive just to bleed again.

With the help of my husband and children, I take it on myself to create what I want from life. Yes, this is a total transformation and I like the new me. However, I am still that little girl with the vivid imagination. I still watch the sunsets and I still hug trees, and time and time again, I try to count the stars. I eat honey all the time, and every day I live, I learn. So my loving family and I create an atmosphere of harmony in our home, to enjoy the love we have for one another.

On 25 September 2013, I had my first book launch, for *The Woman from Brazil*. Author House UK Ltd in the USA published the book on 7 August 2013. The Africa Media House team executed a remarkable project that will make me proud for the rest of my life. Dr Don Mattera, a recipient of many international awards, gave a remarkable narration of my book. Dr Mattera also introduced me as an author to the world of literature. Later that night, I was surprised with a designer birthday cake that looked like a book. My 73-year-old mother, friends, family, business people, and lovers of literature were present to celebrate with me. All of this came to pass, and to think, years back I wanted to take my life.

Let's face it—there is no middle ground between freedom and slavery. So from now on, that is my oath and my sacred law. I am now out of the web of deception and I am free because I have conquered my initial fear—my toxic past. So with my now-meaningful life, I will touch the lives of others as I embrace my own distinctiveness. There is no need for me to try and unravel the mystery of my origin. I no longer care who my father was; all I know is that I am here and I am part of this world—this universe. Firstly, the quest for human dignity should never be questioned. Secondly, I am a human being who belongs to this planet and I am dignified no matter what.

In spite of all the changes in my life, my new dream is starting now, and it will put me on the ultimate journey as it is a legacy and I am on it. In short, my world is wide because I have exposed *the file that was hidden at the bottom*. That file held the inventory of my life, which I now own—it is my basis in fact. The truth is, I took the ruins and made something positive out of it and convinced myself that nothing can be too bad that I cannot change. My mind will no longer be intoxicated with decay. I fed the good seed all my life and killed the toxic past to make way for a new future. With a better future that I see as a safe haven, I commemorate life and only see the landmark of victory. The question is, will I ever understand what happened and why it happened in my past? The answer is no—I will never understand. But, I am proud that I rose to all the challenges, no matter how painful. As a matter of fact, the full truth is still hanging in a vacuum because I never met my father. But maybe he sees me from behind the curtain of time. Who can tell? What I know is what I know, and it provides a sense of absolute abundance for me. I have learnt that in this life we bleed to survive and then we survive just to bleed again. Every day we are at war, and as for me, I refuse to collapse. Instead, I stand like a warrior and fight. Nevertheless, as warriors of our time, we can alleviate the suffering within by accepting the things we cannot change. Life will always have many obstacles that are way beyond our control. Since the question is still hanging, do I have closure? The answer is yes and no, but what I do know for sure is that it is all in the sea of forgetfulness for me. Life is precious, and I exist to enjoy the gift of it. But now that you know my story, I kindly ask you to pray for me to continue to feed the good seed and to remain humble.

So as I sign off, I am glad to know that I have passed with great distinction, with the result I am the signatory of my own report card. The truth is, my toxic past was my school. Therefore, my long-overdue account is settled in full. Hail to myself, for I have broken the chains of my past and have abandoned the walls of its prison. For this reason, I now become blood of my blood and my body the dynamics of my heart. After all, I have rescued my mind from the battle of an abyss. The sacrifice is done and my prize I hold in my hand —I call it my jubilee. In closing, my journey continues.

Never and never become the emotional hostage of your own mind.

Warrior Zuzu


Time is no respecter of person and history does not edit its recordings. It is what it is and so it shall be.

Warrior Zuzu


Become the CEO of your own life and you won't have to beg for attention of extension from anyone.

Warrior Zuzu

# EPILOGUE

First of all, I know that my story is not the worst case in point. But it is a story and it is my reality. Therefore, I acknowledge that there are many out there who are worse off in this world with many complications. But to let you know, I never imagined that it would be the flashbacks of my *toxic past* that would be the perpetrator. Needless to say, that perpetrator has violated and traumatized me for many years. It has taken my rights to live as a human. As a matter of fact, I was antagonized by it when I was that little girl, then that grown woman. However, now that grown woman took her stand. The fact is, that very past made me the emotional hostage of my own mind. Nonetheless, it made me see my dream again. We all have many dreams and goals that we want to accomplish before we leave the earth. For years I followed my dream. Many times I had to put it on hold because of the lack of skills. Sometimes we take things head on but then the timing is wrong. I believe, when the timing is wrong, then one's mental outlook is not yet properly transformed. I waited for the day and the time to connect with that dream— because every beginning has an end. Guess what? My dream was to assassinate my toxic past, and I did because I wanted to and because I could. No one could do it for me. I was the only person authorized by myself to execute the project. So writing this book was not an easy undertaking for me.

This project I put on hold for a while to write two other books, *Broken Face* and *The Woman from Brazil*. These are also about the painful stories of women who persevered and endured the painful eras of their lives. Subsequently, I cried with these women while I interviewed them. In point of fact, I had to get into their shoes, become the first person in order to write about them. Momentary, it was an excursion on its own, and I am happy that through their experiences, I too have learned to appreciate the gift of life. Let's face it—one will never know what another goes through if one is not in their world.

To summarize, when I returned to my memoir, I received healing as I was writing page by page through my tears. During this experience, I have learnt not to only break even, but to break free. Not only am I free, I will not be lured back into the bottomless pit again. The nagging consciousness of wanting to know my family tree I have dismissed. I took my life back from a past that was a hindrance to my soul, my mind and my well-being. Now I am the legal owner of a history that is mine—no matter how toxic. I cannot change my history but my history has changed me—for the better. Now this book is the detail of the odyssey of my life. Furthermore, the time

I had the dialog with my past was incredible. I was alone and I spoke loud and with great aggression. So what I am saying is, never make peace with your toxic past—kill it before it kills you.

However, I don't think we can ever succeed in writing the real feelings of abuse because these are beyond our human explanation. I am not sure but I do not think anyone can really explain with the correct emotion or even the words. You alone know what it's like to stand in that dark place. You are alone and you fear your own thoughts. The overall feeling is, you feed the fear, not knowing that the fear will destroy you. It would seem logical to think that there are many Annie Anonymas out there. They hide behind the curtain, with the invisible masks on their faces. Meanwhile they are silent without a platform while they secretly bleed. They carry on with their lives while the toxic past carries on antagonizing them. They remain the residents of a dark and lonely place. Therefore the purpose of sharing my story is to let them know—life is not over. I hope that those in a similar position will later release themselves from their painful era. This is something only the recipient can do. Take time to ask yourself what makes you hold on to something so painful when you can break free. For one, you think of the many people you are going to hurt, forgetting how you are hurting. What about the scandal of the family secrets that you are exposing? So what? Who, for one, is blameless in this life and without sin? Do what you have to do to free yourself from that sin that you have never created. The fact of the matter is, civilization is sometimes about discrimination, and there is nothing noble about that. We all bleed when we are pulled into a war, but the challenge is how we would stand like warriors and fight to survive. I know for a fact that not everyone will like my work and not everyone will like me, for that matter. However, that is not my concern because I am used to those who so easily give out unrefined words with the intention to damage. As a rule, my rule—I refuse to yield to anything that will incarcerate my mind. In truth, I have been there and will never go back there again. The crux of the matter is, stop suffering and snap out of this awful nightmare where you have no voice.

Nevertheless, in my own words to myself, I invested the power of faith and the love I have for myself. Going back into my past was not easy for me, but it gave me an opportunity to heal and to forgive. In any case, I managed to let go. In whatever way, I can be criticized for saying what I am saying but maybe someone out there might just relate. Nonetheless, there were many days I wanted to give up and rid myself of this manuscript. But a powerful force was present, and it pushed me to go ahead. I realized then that I am not strong the way I thought I would always be. I am only flesh and blood and very far from perfect.

I wrote this book with so many tears as I was going back into my soul. I stepped into another dimension—a place I never thought existed. I am an adult and yet I became a child. In this dimension, I saw myself in pigtails and with blistered hands, gazing at the sunset. I saw the little girl changing the wheel of the Mazda van. I saw Annie watering her garden and speaking to her yellow cling peach tree. But I broke down when I saw little Annie's tears after the hiding with the black genuine-leather belt. As I looked on, the adult tears of Zuzu were falling because I heard her screams of apology. I heard her trembling voice asking God when he will free her from this horrible life. It was painful to go back there but I had to in order to hold on to the sound powers of my mind and to free myself.

As for the scars from that tennis racket, I daily see them on my mother's arms. Surely, I still feel a cold chill running down my spine when I think that those scars were going to be on my face. I don't want to sound vain but I know God protected me on that dark and painful day. To say the least, going back to all those scenarios was like opening up an old infected wound.

Many times I took a break from my computer and just cried like I cried when I was that little child. Verily, I cried many tears in my life, but the tears I cried while writing this book were the tears God wanted me to cry. It was spiritual and my redemption because I know I've made a peaceful offering to myself. This offering is my ideology, and I am equipping with a great treasure of knowing that I belong to the universe. I took this project on, not to praise my toxic past but to assassinate it—and I did. In point, I do not know what the future holds for me but I do know that I am free. It is true that my future is taken care of by a higher authority.

It takes a person with a sane mind to feed and nurture the good seed. By doing so, you become the master of your own thoughts. You work through the processes of guilt, anger, revenge, and hatred. Then finally you learn to say sorry and rid yourself of the hostile and obnoxious behaviours you developed to defend yourself. It is a long painful journey and it is not an easy road to travel on. Despite anything, I had to repeat by rote and believe in my mind that I can do it, but it was never easy. But do take note that it is never too late to start taking back your life.

I recall how I even tried to end my life back in high school with a handful of pills, but even that could not end my agony. I was tired of fighting a war on my own. A war only time could end, is what I thought. I dare to say I tried to push time, not knowing then, time has no special friends. I could not manipulate time because time is always on time. It was not my time to die. Now I know, I was predestined to be on the road to complete my journey and find my destiny. Can I go as far as to say I am here to do my time? To put it differently, I may say that I was a warrior of my time and in my time.

Gradually, that beginning did reach its end, and I have most of the answers I was yearning for. Now that I am free and life has new meaning, I cannot help but give gratitude for many things. For example, my stepfather is the only man I know who has raised me. He was the man that bought me my first bicycle. He taught me to drive a car, do mechanical work, and mow the lawn. Over and above, I now have the skills of gardening and I can take pride in the many things I can do. Simultaneously, I have a good husband who in addition taught me building construction skills and how to handle business. My toxic childhood has groomed me into who I am today—and in a good way. My situation has taught me how to remain positive and to love life. It is not hard for me to dismiss what I am not happy about, and I cherish this idea of a new mindset. Therefore, I cannot help but think that above all, I am most richly blessed, and for every blessing, I give gratitude.

I am at peace with myself now, and it is a fact that I love myself hard enough. It is not something I am just saying because it sounds right. There is no need for me to crave for attention of extension from anyone, no reason to live up to the expectations of others from me. The truth is, our competition with humans will always be fierce. All I know is that I am liberated and I refuse to suffer the indignity of what I never created. Above all, a higher authority and not the thoughts of others guide my life. I believe that all the hurt is slowly fading away. All the tears I cried have dried up—I try to forget why I shed them. With a massive respect, I salute you, the reader, for reading the story of a woman who was desperately seeking closure and transformation. I highly appreciate your time and effort in doing so. As for the people who are my family, they remain that way—my family.

Like I mentioned in this book, we all have a memoir. The writing of that memoir started on the day we entered into this world. The preface started when we were conceived in private, and the day we die, then the memoir is complete. But the memory and legacy may live on until the earth is no more. We all have a story to tell. Sadly, some people refuse to share their story, forgetting that someone out there may need it. The truth is, someone can relate to it and find solace in it. Some might find a strategic guideline for direction and peace of mind from it. Your story might help someone to heal and get moral and emotional strength. There is no doubt that your story will be important to someone and it will have meaning. We are all here on this earth for a reason, and our lives have purpose. All we need to do is sit down and reflect and stop ourselves from crying. Stop the pause of what you know; spread your wings and fly.

My story made me find myself as I adhered to the duty of endurance. I triumph with forgiveness and mount myself like an eagle to fly above all circumstances. I pray that my story would give someone, anyone a ray of hope out there.

That is why I appreciate Renda Rose Williams for sharing her story with the world, in her book *God's Grace and Mercy Brought Me Home*. After reading a few pages,

I cried and closed the book; it was too painful. That's when I read the words on the cover: 'Don't cry for me. I am free.' Later, I managed to read the book until the end. Her story made me realize that my story is but a drop in the ocean. But her story opened a door for me to write about my hidden pain and rid myself of a toxic past. That is why I dedicate this book to Renda Rose Williams, because today I too can say to you *don't cry for me—I am free*. Renda's history was her school. Today she is a motivational speaker and a phenomenal lady who holds many offices, and she did motivate me to break the silence.

I urge you to never fear to share your story, no matter how toxic it may be, because your life story contains the history of your soul. Your soul is what is valuable to God. You might fear that people will know who you are and where you come from. But bear in mind, those who live in glass houses dare not throw stones. What people say or think of you is for their consideration. The constant criticisms of others are only there to make you grow and find the depth within yourself. That which you fear—let it become the beginning of your wisdom. What is important is that you walk the earth and one day you will leave the earth. The very fact of your existence is what matters. Do not allow the truth to be dressed with a raincoat—set it free. Then people won't throw it in your face anymore. In fact, you will be seen as that person that walks with confidence and a brazen assurance. Know that the past only prepares us to enter into the future. The hand of God always guides the future. As for me, my future belongs to me now because I chose to be free and not a victim. For now, I am in my calling as a warrior and I will be submissive to the duty of my calling.

In conclusion, it is vital for you to know that you are special and you have a purpose for being here. Meaning is what one carves out of life for us. All you have to do is look for the frontiers of all possibilities. That is how we become the stewards of our own destiny in a world of many obstacles. To emphasize, seek for truth and it will find you. Be honest with yourself and the way you feel. Confess that which you fear to yourself, and it will not have a hold on you anymore. In ending, my toxic past has made me a warrior of my time. Therefore, I urge you to step into your greatness because you are special, and let the world read about your soul.

Warrior Zuzu

# AUTHOR'S NOTE

I pray that you, the reader, will forgive me for any repetition but I write what comes to heart in the moment, through my tears.

# Meet Me

Hello, everybody, remember me, or don't you know me anymore?

Not that I care because really I don't. Why, because you know what you do with me. Here you are without a clue of who I am, forgetting that sometimes you love me and sometimes you don't. If I can refresh your mind, there are many occasions when you abuse me, disrespect me, and then you use me to lie to others and yourself. You play with me yet I am not interested what you do with me. You sometimes regret that you have lost me. Then you try to make up with me again, not that I mind. However, what you do with me does not concern me. I don't care about you and what you do because I am no respecter of person. I have no enemies and no friends. Who you are, what you have, and where you come from is not my concern. The games you play have no effect on me. In truth, what you feel for me is what you feel. You conduct deceit and lies in my name, thinking that you are proficient in what you do. Only you will regret it because you are the mastermind with the games that you play in my name. You are the one amusing yourself with what you do when you disrespect me. I am always there for you but you think you can fool with me—you fool yourself. You waste your own life while I walk on by.

Tell me who I am. You know me but now you don't. Let me introduce myself once again. Hello everybody, my name is Time—don't play with me.

Warrior Zuzu